Woman in Modern Society

Women in Modern Society

Earl Barnes

VANI

Creative Imprint of Vani Prakashan

VANI

4695, 21-A, Daryaganj, New Delhi 110 002

Branch

Ashok Rajpath, Patna 800 004

Phone : +91 11 23273167 Fax : +91 11 23275710

www.vaniprakashan.in
vaniprakashan@gmail.com

WOMEN IN MODERN SOCIETY
by Earl Barnes

ISBN: 978-93-5000-949-9
Criticism

First Edition

Price : ₹ 350

Printed at Thomson Press, Delhi 110 020

Vani Prakashan's signature motif is created by Artist Maqbool Fida Husain

THIS VOLUME IS DEDICATED TO A WOMAN

end by her ancestors with heath and strength,
reared by a wise mother,
trained to earn her own living, and university bred,
at one time an independent wage-earner
and now equal partner in the business of a home,
a social force in the life of her community,
member of a woman's club,
a suffragist,
the devoted and intelligent mother of a group o f
fine children,
and the centre of a family which loves and
reverences her
and finds the deepest meaning of life in her
presence.

Contents

What it Means to be a Woman

WE GO back to the earliest forms of life, where the unit is simply a minute mass of protoplasm surrounded by a cell wall, we find each of these divisions to be a complete individual. It can feed itself, that its life may go on today; it can fight or run away, that it may be here to fight tomorrow; and by a process of division it can create a new life so that its existence may continue across the generations. With such units it is quite conceivable that life might go on through all eternity, death following birth, were it not that protoplasm contains within itself a principle of change. Life and change are synonymous.

And this change moves ever toward a complexity, which we call development, where cells unite in a larger life, and functions and organs are specialised. Thus there comes a time when the part split off carries with it power to eat and digest, to fight or run away, but only half the power of procreation. This half unit, this incomplete individual, is either male or female, and from this time on, the epic of life gathers around the search of these half-lives for their complements. The force that impels to this search, while at first valuable only for the perpetuation of the generations, gathers into itself modifying feeling and desires and, at a later period, ideas and ideals, which finally, when men and women appear, make it the greatest of all the shaping forces in life.1

Of course, in such a sweeping statement as this, one must include under sex hunger all the forces that drive men and women to seek each other's society, rather than that of their own sex. In this sense, it can be truly said that it gives a motive for our care of offspring, and for all our other most self-forgetful devotions, our finest altruisms, our most polished expressions in language, manners and dress. It justifies labour, ambition, and at times even self-effacement. It underlies nearly all the lyric expressions in art; furnishes almost the only theme for that delineation of modern life which we call the novel; and is a main support for music, painting, statuary and belles-lettres. It gives us the institution of the family, which is the parent of the state; it is closely allied to religion; and in our individual lives it lifts us to the heights of self-realisation and happiness, or plunges us down to the depths of degradation and tragedy.

While this sex hunger belongs equally to men and women, it has come to be associated with women, until we even speak of them as "the sex." Hence, when we are discussing women, we are generally discussing the sex interest common to both men and women, and this disturbs our point of view. The fact is that sex interest is a common possession, that the unit in human life, even more than among lower animals, is always a male and a female bound together by love. Just as a body can function in sleep or under the influence of a narcotic, for a time seemingly independent of the mind, so a man or a woman can live for a time in seeming independence of the opposite sex; but from any biological point of view, such a separate existence of male and female is only a transient effort. The half-life must find its mate or, after a few brief days, it dies, leaving its line extinct. For all the larger purposes of life, man is but a half-creature, and woman is equally a fragment.

It is, of course, conceivable that these two halves of the biological unit might have been made, or might have developed, alike in everything except the sexual function. At least they might have been as much alike as men are alike. They might have been of the same sise, possessed of the same strength, of the same figures and gestures, complexion and hair. Their voices might have been alike. They might have had the same kinds of nervous systems, with the same desires, feelings, ideas and tendencies. In the assertions and arguments born of intellectual, industrial, social and political readjustments, it is often assumed that this is the case. Differences are minimised or denied, and an attempt is made to resolve the world of men and women into a world of human beings capable of living together in mingled competitions and cooperations, regardless of sex, except where the reproductive process is considered. But this view is superficial; born of argument it breaks down when confronted by any body of significant facts.

Again, it has happened that in the long struggle of developing civilisation, sometimes one and sometimes the other sex has gained what has seemed an advantage over the other, just as in the development of any man's individual life, his brain may gain a seeming advantage over his stomach, so that it has more than its fair share of nourishment and activity. Arguing from such a case, we might declare the brain superior to the stomach in power, health and function; but in the long accounting, all such temporary superiorities are wiped out. So with men and women, seeming advantages for either are gained only at the expense of the common life; and in the last analysis, each finds his individual value only in the common life of the unit.

Let us try then to see what the special characteristics of women are, ignoring as far as possible the accidental variations of individuals, and the temporary advantages or disadvantages due to economic or ideational forces, and all assertions of what would be if things were not as they are.

While the whole matter of sex differences is in a state of unsettlement, it seems very certain that males are more active and more variable than females. This superabundant vitality appears in the males of the higher animals in secondary sex characteristics, such as more abundant and unnecessary hair and feathers, tusks, spurs, antlers, wattles, brilliant colors and scent pouches. It also appears in mating calls, songs, and general carriage of the body. Correspondingly, the female is smaller, duller coloured, and less immediately attractive than the male.

All the studies that have been made on men and women, also confirm our ordinary observation that men are taller, heavier, stronger and more active than women, and this holds true in all stages of civilisation, wherever tests have been made. In strength, rapidity of movement, and rate of fatigue Miss Thompson's studies[2] show that men have a very decided advantage over women. Thus in strength tests, the men in Yale have double the power of women in Oberlin;**3** while our college athletic records place men far ahead of women in all events requiring strength and endurance.

The differences in structure between men and women are such as to correspond with the functional differences just stated. A woman's bones are smaller in proportion to her size, than are those of a man. The body is longer, the hips broader, and the abdomen more prominent. Relatively to the length of the body, the arms, legs, feet and hands are shorter than in men, the lower leg and arm are shorter in proportion to the upper leg and arm. Man has the long levers and the active frame. One has only to look at two good statues of a man and a woman to realise the greater strength and activity of the man.

Woman, as she actually appears in modern society, is also less subject to variation than man;**4** she is much less liable to be a genius or an idiot than her brother.**5** She offers greater resistance to disease, endures pain and want more stoically, and lives longer; so that while more boys than girls are born in all parts of the world, where statistics are kept, in mature years women always outnumber men.

All these statements are summed up by saying that not only in women, but in most female animals of the higher orders, life is more anabolic than in males. They tend to more static conditions; they collect, organise, conserve; they are patient and stable; they move about less; they more easily lay on adipose tissue. Compared with the female, the male animal is katabolic; he is active, impulsive, destructive, skilful, creative, intense, spasmodic, violent. Such a generalisation as this must not be pushed too far in its applications to our daily life; but as a statement of basal differences it seems justified by ordinary observation as well as by scientific tests.**6**

Meantime, it is probably true that the female, as mother of the race, is more important biologically than the male, since she both furnishes germ plasm and nourishes the newly conceived life. The latest studies, along lines laid down by Mendel, seem to indicate that the female brings to the new creation both male and female attributes, while the male brings only male qualities. Thus when either sex sinks into insignificance, as sometimes happens in lower forms of life, it is generally the male which exists merely for purposes of reproduction.**7**

The differences in the nervous systems of men and women are now fairly established on the quantitative side. Marshall has shown that if we compare brain weight with the stature in the two sexes there is a slight preponderance of cerebrum in males; but if the other parts of the brain are taken into consideration, the sexes are equal.**8** Havelock Ellis has carefully gathered the results of many investigators and declares that woman's brain is slightly superior to man's in proportion to her size.**9** But these quantitative differences are now felt to have comparatively little significance; and of the relative qualities of the brain substance in the two sexes we know nothing positively. In fact, if we give a scientist a section of brain substance he cannot tell whether it is the brain of a man or a woman.

It is very probable that the average woman's mind is capable of much the same activity as the average man's mind, given the same heredity and the same training. They are both alike capable of remarkable feats of imitation, and an ordinarily intelligent man could probably learn to wear woman's clothes, and walk as she generally walks, so as to deceive even a jury of women, if there were a motive to justify the effort. Women also can perform, and they do perform, most of the feats of men.

At the same time it is desirable to note present differences in modes of thinking and feeling, for while they may have been produced by environment and ideals, and may hence give way to education, they must be reckoned with in making the next steps. In the chapter on education we shall discuss certain academic peculiarities of women's minds, but here we are interested in seeing what fundamental differences characterise the thinking of the sexes.

Women seem more subject to emotional states than men;**10** and this general observation agrees with the fact that the basal ganglia of the brain are more developed in women than in men, and these parts of the brain seem most intimately concerned with emotional activity. Whether emotion follows acts or leads to acts remains a disputed question, but certainly emotion gives charm and significance to life and distinguishes modes of thinking. Particularly in the dramatic art, this quality of mind gives women special excellence. The fact that she more often appeals to emotion than to reason, as cause for action, in no way marks her as inferior to man, but simply as different. As Ellen Key says: "There is nothing more futile than to try to prove the inferiority of woman to man, unless it be to try to prove her equality."**11**

Most women think in particulars as compared with men. The individual circumstance seems to them very important; and it is hard for them to get away from the concrete. On the other hand, a man's thinking is more impersonal and general; and he is more easily drawn into abstractions. It is true that woman's domestic life would naturally develop this quality but we are not now concerned with the question of origins. Most women find it easy to live from day to day; the man is more given to systematising and planning. Thus in offices, men are more efficient as heads of departments, while women handle details admirably. In public life we have recently seen thousands of women eager to depose a United States Senator, accused of polygamy, without regard to the bearing of the concrete act on constitutional guarantees. Women have done little with abstract studies like metaphysics; they have done much with the novel, where ideas are presented in the concrete and particular.

This habit of dealing with particulars, and disinclination for abstraction, leads easily to habitual action. It is easy for women to stock up their lower nerve centres with reflex actions. This, of course, goes along with the general anabolic characteristics of the sex. Hence women are the conservers of traditions; rules of conducting social intercourse appeal to them; and they are the final supporters of theological dogmas.**12** Women naturally uphold caste, and Daughters of the Revolution and Colonial Dames flourish on the scantiest foundations of ancestral excellence. Man, on the other hand, is more radical and creative. He has perfected most of our inventions; he has painted our great pictures; carved our great statues; he has written music, while women have interpreted it.

Along with these fixed qualities of action, women have a tendency to indirection when they advance. We say they have diplomacy, tact and coquetry, while man is more direct and bald in his methods. Of course, one easily understands how these qualities may have arisen, since "fraud is the force of weak natures," and woman has always been driven to supplement her weakness with tact, from the days of Jael and Delilah down to the present day adventuress.

These qualities of mind naturally drive women to literary interests which are concrete, personal and emotional. Men turn more easily than women to the abstract generalisations of science. Of course, there are marked exceptions to these general statements, in both sexes. Madame Curie, who was recently a candidate for the honours of the French Academy, and who, in 1911, was given the Nobel prise for her distinguished services to chemistry, is but one of many women who are famous today in the world of science. Still the private life of these women, as in the case of Sónya Kovalévsky, seems to bear out our general conclusion. Men, on the other hand, as milliners and editors of ladies' journals, show marked skill in catering to women's tastes; but on the whole the differences indicated seem important and widely diffused.

Another profound difference between men and women is the woman's greater tendency to periodicity in all her functions and adjustments to life.**13** In all normal societies the life of the man is fairly regular and constant from birth to old age. He moves along lines mainly predetermined by his heredity and his environment, his habits and his work. Even puberty is less disturbing in its effect upon a boy than upon a girl; and often by eighteen we can anticipate the life of a young man with great accuracy. The one element in his life hardest to forecast is the effect of his love-affairs.

With a woman, it is quite different. As a girl, the period of puberty produces profound changes; and after that, for more than thirty years she passes through periodical exaltations and depressions that must play a large part in determining her health, happiness and efficiency. In the forties, comes another great change which affects her life to a degree strangely ignored by those who have dealt with her possibilities in the past.**14**

But the great element of uncertainty, always fronting the girl and young woman, is marriage. Marriage for her generally means abandonment of old working interests, and a substitution of new; it brings her geographical change; new acquaintances and friendships; and the steady adjustment of her personal life to the man she has married in its relation to industry, religion, society and the arts. If children come to her, they must inevitably retire her from public life, for a time, with the danger of losing connections which comes to all who temporarily drop out of the race.

A boy, industrious, observant, with some power of administration, studies mining engineering, moves to a mining centre and expresses his individual and social powers along the lines of his work until he is sixty. The women who impinge against his life may deflect him from the mines in California to those in Australia, or from the actual work of superintendence to an office; or from an interest in Browning to Tennyson; or from Methodism to Christian Science. The girl with industrious and observant interests studies stenography and typewriting, moves to the vicinity of offices, but is then caught up in the life of a farmer-husband who shifts her centre of activity to a farm in Idaho where she must devote herself to entirely different activities, form new associations, think in new terms, respond to new emotions, and adjust herself to her farmer-husband's personality. When, after twenty-five years, she has reared a family of children, and when improved circumstances enable them to move up to the county seat, she confronts many of the conditions for which she originally prepared herself, but with farm habits, diminishing adaptability and diminishing power of appealing to her husband. His powers are still comparatively unimpaired, and as a dealer in farm produce or farm machinery his interests undergo slight change. In general, it may be said that a woman's life falls into three great periods of twenty-five years each. The first twenty-five years of childhood and girlhood is a time of getting ready for the puzzling combination of her personal needs as a human being, her needs as a self-supporting social unit, and her probabilities of matrimony. The second twenty-five years, the domestic period of her life, is a time of adjustments as wife and mother, which may instead prove to be a period of barren waiting, or a time of professional and industrial self-direction and self-support. The third twenty-five years is a time of mature and ripened powers, of lessened romantic interests, and if the preceding period has been devoted to husband and children, it is often a time of social detachment, of weakened individual initiative, of old-fashioned knowledge, of inefficiency, of premature retirement and old age.

On the moral side, as Professor Thomas has so admirably pointed out,**15** women have evolved a morality of the person and of the family, while men have evolved a morality of the group and of property. Since men have had a monopoly of property and of law-making they have shaped laws mainly for the protection of property, and in a secondary degree for the protection of the person. Under these laws a man who beats another nearly to death is less severely punished than one who signs the wrong name to a check for five dollars. Man's katabolic nature and his greater freedom have given him almost a monopoly of crime under these laws which he has made. Offences against the coming generation, against health, social efficiency and good taste have until recently been left to the tribunal of public opinion as expressed in social usage; and here, as we have seen, women are generally the judges and executioners. In this, her own field of moral judgement, woman is idealistic and uncompromising. If one of her sisters falls from virtue she will often pursue her unmercifully. If a man, on the other hand, commits a burglary or forgery her sympathy and mercy may make her a very lenient judge.

In aesthetics, the differences follow the same general law. Women express beauty in themselves; jewels are for their ornament; and rooms are furnished as a setting for themselves. The lives of millions of workers go to the adornment of women. In painting they sometimes excel, but a Madame Le Brun does her best work when she paints herself and her child, and when Angelica Kauffmann would paint a vestal virgin, she drapes a veil over her own head and transfers her features to the canvas. Sculpture and architecture are too impersonal and abstract to attract much attention from women at present. Even a sculptor like Mrs. Bessie Potter Vonnoh finds her truest theme in statuettes of mothers with their children about them.

During the past few years psychologists have paid great attention to secondary sex characteristics of the mind, and doubtless many qualities of the thought and feeling of men and women owe their origin to the same source as brilliant plumage, antlers, combs and wattles. Thus the shy, retiring, reticent, self-effacing, languishing, adoring excesses of maidenhood and the peculiar psychological manifestations of the late forties must probably be understood from this point of view. So, also, must the bold, swaggering, assertive, compelling bearing of youth be interpreted. The shy or modish, dandified, lackadaisical cane-carrying youth is naturally disliked as a sexual perversion.

Women alone, whether individually or in groups, tend to develop certain hard, dry, arid qualities of mind and heart, or they become emotional and unbalanced. Losing a sense of large significances, they become overcareful, saving, sometimes penurious, while in matters of feeling they lavish sentiment and sympathy on unimportant pets and movements.

Men, when alone, become selfish, coarse, and reckless; their judgements become extravagant and their pursuits remorseless.

Thus it is certainly true that men and women supplement each other in the subjective as in the objective life. Man creates, woman conserves; man composes, woman interprets; man generalises, woman particularises; man seeks beauty, woman embodies beauty; man thinks more than he feels, woman feels more than she thinks. For new spiritual birth, as for physical birth, men and women must supplement each other.

To be a woman then, is to be for twenty-five years a girl and then a young woman, capable of feeding and protecting herself, possessed of preparing and conserving powers superior to her brothers. After that, for twenty-five years, she is a human being primarily devoted to romanticism, finding her largest fulfilment only in wifehood and motherhood, direct or vicarious; in the last twenty-five years, she should be a wise woman, of ripe experience, carrying over her gathered training and powers to the service of the group All this time she is, like the man, an incomplete creature, realising her greatest power and her greatest service only when working in loving association with the man of her choice.

Woman's Hetitage

O THOROUGHLY HAVE modern men fastened their attention upon the problems of the immediate present, that one feels driven to justify oneself in taking up an historical investigation of any subject presented in a popular manner. And yet it takes little argument to show that what we shall be depends in large measure on what we are; and that what we are rests back on what we have been. In anything we try to think or feel or do, we quickly reach a limit; and this limit is determined by the original quality of our nervous system plus the training it has received. For here is the curious fact about this instrument of thought and feeling which at once takes it away from comparison with mechanical instruments. Whatever it does, becomes a part of itself, and then helps to determine what it will do the next time and how it will do it. With the making easy of mental operations through repetition, and with the formation of associations based on our choices, it may be truly said that we become whatever we habitually think and feel and do.

Every choice we make is thus literally built into our character and becomes a part of ourselves. After that, the old choice will help determine the new, and we shall find ourselves being directed by all of our past choices, and even by the choices of our ancestors. Since, then, all our earlier selves are continued in us and make us what we are, we are simply studying ourselves when we study the history of our ancestors. If we would go forward, we must first look backward; for we must rise on stepping-stones of our dead selves.

But history is not merely the story of the past. To relate that, would take as long as it took to live it, and the result would be but weariness of spirit. History, to be significant, must select the events with which it will deal; it must arrange these in series that are in accord with the constitution of things; and then it must use the generalisations it reaches to interpret the present, and even to forecast the future. It is obvious that this interpretation will depend on the point of view held by the interpreter.

Hence we must ask in what fundamental beliefs this presentation rests. These are, first, that life tends to move along certain lines that constitute the law of human nature. Just as the infant tends first to wriggle, then creep, then walk, then run and dance, so human nature tends to move upward from savagery through primitive settled life to the complex forms of larger settled units. In this progress, material or economic forces play a large part; but ideas, originally born out of circumstances, but sometimes borrowed from other people, sometimes degenerate remnants of past utilities, also play a large part. The progress we finally make is thus directed by this human tendency, by material circumstances, and by ideas. Sometimes it keeps pretty closely to what seems to us to be upward human growth; sometimes it stagnates; sometimes it gives us perverted products; and sometimes it destroys itself.

Thus it becomes necessary to trace the past experiences of woman that we may see with what heritage she faces the future. She is all that she has felt and thought and done. She started with at least half of the destiny of the race in her keeping. Handicapped in size and agility, and periodically weighted down by the burdens of maternity, she still possessed charms and was mistress of pleasures which made her, for savage man, the dearest possession next to food; and for civilised man, the companion, joy and inspiration of his days.

Of woman's position in early savage times we know only what we can learn from fragmentary prehistoric remains, from the structure of early languages, from records of travellers and students among savages of more recent times; or what can be inferred from human nature in general. Most of this data is difficult to interpret, but it is probable that woman's position was not much worse than man's. It is a bad beast that fouls its own food or its own nest; and the female had always the protection of the male's desire. If she could not entirely control her body, she could still control her own expressions of affection and desire; and, without these, mere possession lost much of its charm.

As keeper of the cave, cultivator of the soil, and guardian of the child, woman, rather than her more foot-loose mate, probably became the centre of the earliest civilisation. The jealousy of men formed tribal rules for her protection; and to these, religion early gave its powerful sanctions. Thus there came a day when the woman took her mate home to her tribe and gave her children her own name. Even if the matriarchal period was not so important as has sometimes been assumed, woman certainly had large influence over tribal affairs in early savage life.

With the increase in population, and the consequent disappearance of game, man was forced to turn his attention to the crude agriculture which woman had begun to develop The superior qualities which he had acquired in war and the chase, enabled him slowly to improve on these beginnings and to shape a body of custom which made settled society possible. With man's leadership in the family the patriarchal form of government developed, and man's power over woman was sanctioned by custom and law. The woman was stolen, or bought; and while sexual attraction did not play the continuous part which it plays in developed society, it must have done much to protect women from abuse and neglect, at least during the years of girlhood and child-bearing. It is at this point that our historical records begin.

In the pages of Homer, or of the Old Testament, in Tacitus's *Germania*, or in the writings of Livy, we find woman's position well defined. True, she stands second to the man, but she is his assistant, not his slave. She must be courted, and while marriage presents are exchanged, she is not bought. In times of emergency, she steps to the front and legislates, judges, or fights. It is possible in the pages of the Old Testament to find women doing everything which men can do. Even where the power is not nominally in her own hands, she often, as in the cases of Penelope or Esther, rules by indirection. Her body and her offspring are protected; and the Hebrew woman of the Proverbs shows us a singularly free and secure industrial position.**16** Such was the condition in primitive Judea, in early Greece, in republican Rome, or among the Germans who invaded southern Europe in the third and fourth centuries of our era.

Man's jealousy of his woman as a source of pleasure and honour to himself, and to his family, must have always acted to limit woman's freedom, even while it gave her protection and a secure position in society. With the development of settled government in city states, like Athens or early Rome, the necessity for defining citizenship made the family increasingly a political institution. A man's offspring through slave women, concubines, or "strangers" lived outside the citisen group, and so were negligible; but the citizen woman's children were citizens, and so she became a jealously guarded political institution. The established family became the test of civic, military, and property rights. The regulations limiting the freedom of girls and women were jealously enforced, since mismating might open the treasures of citizenship to any low born or foreign adventurer.**17**

In the ancient Orient, in Greece, Rome, and in later Europe, these stages have been repeated again and again. Woman is first a slave, stolen or bought, protected by sexual interest to which is later added social custom and religious sanction. Early civilisation centres around the woman, so that she becomes in some degree the centre of the home-staying group In primitive civilisation man takes over woman's most important activities; but she gains a fixed position, protected, though still further enslaved, by political necessities.

But with the increase of wealth, whether in terms of money, slaves, or trade, woman found herself subject to a fourth form of enslavement more subtly dangerous than brute force, lust, or political and religious institutionalism. This was the desire of man to protect her and make her happy because he loved her. He put golden chains about her neck and bracelets on her arms, clothed her in silks and satins, fed her with dainty fare, gave her a retinue of attendants to spare her fatigue, and put her in the safest rear rooms of the habitation. But it is foolish to talk of conscious enslavement in this connection. Rich men and luxurious civilisations have always enslaved women in the same way that rich, fond, and foolish mothers have enslaved their children, by robbing them of opportunity, by taking away that needful work and that vital experience of real life which alone can develop the powers of the soul.

Thus in the Periclean age in Greece, in the Eastern Kingdoms established by Alexander, in Imperial Rome, in the later Italian Renaissance, in France under Louis XIV and Louis XV, in England under the Stuart kings, and in many centres of our own contemporary world, women have given up their legitimate heritage of work and independent thought for trinkets, silks, and servants, and have quickly degenerated, like the children of rich and foolish mothers, into luxury-loving parasites and playthings.**18**

To maintain this luxurious setting for their mistresses, whether wives or irregular concubines, men of the Occident have generally been driven to ever fiercer struggle with their fellows. Thus a Pericles, at the zenith of his powers, facing difficulties which strained and developed all his forces, had for his legitimate wife a woman, bound hand and foot by conventions and immured in her house in Athens. But a man is only half a complete human being, and the other half cannot be furnished by a weak and ignorant kept-woman, no matter how legal the bond. Hence the forces always driving men to completeness and unity drove Pericles away from his house and his legitimate children and his mere wife to find the completion of his life.

In these cases, as elsewhere, demand creates supply, and there were to be found everywhere in Athens able and cultivated foreign women, many of whom had come over from the mainland of Asia Minor; and one of these, Aspasia, became the mistress of Pericles and bore him children. She was no adventuress of the street, but an educated and brilliant woman, in whose home you might have met not only Pericles, but also Socrates, Phidias, Anaxagoras,

Sophocles and Euripides.

This is the stage that always follows the period of the luxury-loving wife. It was so in Imperial Rome, in later Carthage, in Venice, and in eighteenth-century France. But the normal human unit is the man and woman who love each other, not these combinations of illegality, law, lust, love and dishonour. Such a triangle of two women and a man rests its base in shame, and its lines are lies, and its value is destruction. So virile republican Rome swept over decadent Greece and made it into the Roman province of Achaia; later the chaste Germans swarmed over the decadent Roman Empire and then slowly rebuilt modern Europe; the ascetic Puritans destroyed the Stuarts; while the French Revolution was the deluge that swept away Louis XVI and put the virtuous, if commonplace, bourgeoisie in power.

So far we have dealt with the position of women as though it depended alone on human hungers, passions and environment; but while these are the driving forces of life, they are very subject to the repressing and diverting power of ideas, working in an environment of economic conditions. These ideas may themselves date back to earlier passions and economic conditions, but they often survive the time which created them, and then they enter into life and conduct as seemingly independent forces. These ideas played a large part, even in the ancient world.

The Jews organised their religious and political practices about a patriarchal Deity ruling a patriarchal state; and their tradition handicapped all women with the sin of Eve, the sin of seeking knowledge. The Greeks, on the other hand, gave woman a splendid place in the hierarchy of the gods, and idealised not only her beauty in Aphrodite but her chaste aloofness in Artemis, her physical strength in the Amazons, and her wisdom in Athena and Hera. They covered the Acropolis with matchless monuments in honour of Athena, patron goddess of their fair city, and celebrated splendid pageants on her anniversaries. So, too, republican Rome, while it gathered its civic life about patriarchal ideas in which the father was supreme, gave women positions of high honour in its religion, whether as deities or as servitors of the gods. In the

Niebelungenlied, the Germans bodied forth their splendid conceptions of female beauty, strength and passion in such figures as Brunhilda. These ideas must have done much to offset the physical weakness and functional handicaps of women in the ancient world.

The Christian ideas, which have dominated us now for nearly two thousand years, are generally considered to have been favourable to women. In their insistence on the value of the human soul, and on democratic equality, they have doubtless helped to raise the status of women along with that of all human beings. But, as between man and woman, Christianity has given every possible advantage to men, and has added needlessly to the natural burdens of women.**19**

From Judaism, Christianity borrowed Eve, with her eternally operative sin, and thus placed all women under a perpetual load of suspicion and guilt. The Founder of the new faith never assumed the responsibilities of a family, and he included no woman among his disciples. Example, even negative example, is often more powerful than precept. Paul, the most learned of the disciples, in his writings, and as an organiser of the Church, emphasised the older Jewish position. In the new organisation, women filled only lesser places, while the men settled all points of dogma, directing and mainly conducting the services of worship Meantime each woman's soul remained her own, to be saved only by her individual actions; therein lay her hope for the future, both on earth and in heaven.

But it was those later developments of belief and practice that gathered around Christian asceticism which placed woman and her special functions under a cloud of suspicion from which she is not even yet entirely freed. Celibacy became exalted; virginity was a positive virtue; chastity, instead of a healthful antecedent to parenthood, became an end in itself; and monasteries and convents multiplied throughout Christendom. Something of shame and guilt gathered around conception and birth, as representing a lower standard of life, even when sanctified by the ceremonies of the Church. From the second century to the sixth, the ablest of the

Church Fathers, Greek and Latin alike, formulated statements in which woman became the chief ally of the devil in dragging men down to perdition. We still hear ancestral reverberations of these teachings in all our discussions of woman's place in civilisation.

But ideas can only for a time overcome or divert the primitive human hungers, and slowly Mary, Mother of Jesus, won first place among the saints. Celibate recluses who feared to walk the streets for fear of meeting a woman, and who spent the nights fighting down their noblest passions, starving them, flagellating and rolling their naked bodies in thorny rose hedges or in snow-drifts to silence demands for wife and children, threw themselves in an ecstasy of adoration before an image of the Virgin with the Baby in her arms. So Maryolatry came to bless the world.

But even this blessing was not without alloy, for it gave us an ideal of woman, superhuman, immaculate, bowing in frightened awe before the angel with the lily, standing mute with crossed hands and downcast eyes before her Divine Son. She represented, not the institution of the family, but the institution of the Church. Even when she appeared in representations of the Holy Family, Joseph, her husband, was not the father of her child, but his servant.

Chivalry took up this conception, and shaped for us the fantastic lady who stands back of much of modern romantic love. Robbed of her simple, human, pagan passions, she became often an anaemic and unfruitful, if angelic, creature. For the direct and passionate assurances of a virtuous and noble love she substituted sighs and tears, languishing looks and weary renunciations. This sterile hybrid, bred of human passions and theological negations, must be finally banished from our literature and from our minds before we can have a healthy eugenic conscience among us.**20**

The Protestant Revolution went far to restore the special functions of women to respect. Belief in her individual soul, and in its need of salvation through individual choice, was supplemented by the belief that this choice must be guided by her individual judgement. Celibacy ceased to be a sign of righteousness; and the best men and women married. But beliefs cannot be directly destroyed by revolution; they can only be disturbed and modified.

The teachings of Paul, Augustine, Tertullian and St Jerome were still authoritative, and Calvin and Knox reaffirmed many of them. The family was still subordinate to the Church; and marriage still remained a sacrament, with theological significances, rather than the simple union of a man and woman who loved each other. The choice of a mate once made was final, because theological, and it could be broken only with infinite pain and disgrace.

The great political upheaval, which we call the French Revolution, carried in its fundamental teachings freedom and opportunity for men and for women; but like the corresponding revolution in religion, it required time to make adjustments, and so we have been content to live for more than a hundred years in the midst of verbal affirmations which we denied in all our institutional life.

In America, conditions have always been favourable for women to work out their freedom. Among the immigrants who came to our shores before 1840 there were, of course, a few traders, adventurers and servants who hoped to improve their financial conditions; but the leaders, and most of the rank and file, came that they might be free to think their own thoughts and live their own lives. If this selection of colonists, through religious and political persecution, sometimes gave us bigots with one idea, it also gave us people who knew that ideas can change. Along with Cotton Mather it gave us Anne Hutchinson, Roger Williams and William Penn.

Most of these who came in the early days belonged to extreme dissenting sects believing in salvation through individual choice, based on personal judgements. Preaching was exalted at the expense of ritual; and by substituting new thinking for old habits in religion, the American settlers made it less difficult for other adjustments to be made, even in such a conservative matter as woman's position. It is through no accident that Methodists, Friends, Unitarians and the Salvation Army have been much more sympathetic to woman's progress than have the older ritualistic faiths.

And these theological ideas had to be worked out under the

material conditions of the New World, which were also favourable to the emancipation of women. Facing primitive conditions in the forest, it became a habit to do new things in new ways. Woman's work and judgement were indispensable; and these picked women showed themselves capable in every direction. They did every kind of work; and when it came to enduring privation or even to starving, they set an example for men.

But while every new movement in ideas always carries with it other radical ideas, the practical difficulties of mental, social and legal adjustment always prevent the full and harmonious development of all that is involved in any new point of view. In the American colonies the need for new adjustments in religion, government and practical living made it inevitable that any very important change in woman's position should linger. In fact, the student of colonial records finds many traces of ultra conservatism in the treatment of women, though the forces had been liberated which must inevitably open the way for her through the New World of America into a new world of the spirit.

And before the quickening influence of the new life had time to become commonplace, the struggle with England began. The Revolutionary period was a time of intense political education for every one. War and sacrifice glorified the new ideas; and even the children and women could not escape their influence. Why then did not the American Revolution pass on to full freedom and opportunity for women? For the same reason that it did not forever abolish slavery in America. The vested interests involved were so many, and the changes so momentous and difficult, that only the most imperative needs could receive attention.

But this does not mean that the interest in a larger life for women was not active or that women were making no advance in self-direction. There is evidence that women like Abigail Adams realised the abstract injustice of their position, and the fact that as early as 1794, Mary Wollstonecraft's *Vindication of the Rights of Woman* was republished in Philadelphia shows that her ideas must have had some currency in America.

After the Revolution, the intimate, stimulating influence of

Europe, which the earlier colonists had enjoyed, was for a time almost entirely lost. The new States became extremely provincial; and minds untouched by the larger world always tend to conservatism. Noah Webster, in "A Letter to Young Ladies," published in Boston in 1790, declared that they "must be content to be women; to be mild, social and sentimental." Three years later the "Letters to a Young Lady," by the Reverend John Bennett, were republished in Philadelphia, after going through several London editions. He placed the qualities to be cultivated in this order: "A genteel person, a simple nature, sensibility, cheerfulness, delicacy, softness, affability, good manners, regular habits, skill in fancy work, and a fund of hidden genteel learning." Through the first half of the nineteenth century these ideals struggled along parallel with the new ideas that were everywhere springing up from the colonial forest experiences of the last two generations.

As conservers of morals and as leaders in higher ideals of life, the advanced women of America came early face to face with two outgrown abuses. One of these was human slavery and the other was intemperance. In attacking these abuses, women had to break with all the traditions that defined their position.

The wealthy and intelligent Englishwoman, Frances Wright, who came to this country in 1818 to attack slavery, found herself doubly opposed because she was a woman speaking in public. Had not St Paul declared: "It is a shame for women to speak in the church"? Lucretia Mott, born in the Society of Friends in Nantucket, had escaped the full force of this injunction, but even she found, when she attacked slavery in public, that she had invaded a world sacred to men, and she was sternly warned back. Miss Susan B Anthony also began her public life as a teacher and a temperance reformer. It was only when she found herself helpless, in presence of the prejudices against her sex, that she turned her attention to freeing women from all purely sex limitation in public life.

When the Civil War broke out, the women were ready to do their part. It is quite possible that the names of Clara Barton and Dorothea Dix may be remembered when Grant and Sherman are forgotten. With the establishing of new human values the historian of the future may consider the saving of life and the preventing of misery as more worthy of lasting record than even military genius. These women and their millions of helpers had not the resources of organised government at their disposal; but, instead, they had oftentimes to work against the jealousy of those in authority. At the close of the war, the Sanitary Commission comprised seven thousand aid societies scattered over the country, and it had raised over fifteen millions of dollars. Those women who remained at home, in the absence of fathers and sons for four years, faced all the problems of practical life. Who can estimate the value of training in cooperative work and organisation which the Civil War gave to the American women?

In the Civil War, women directly served men; but in the great industrial reorganisation which came afterward they served mainly women and children. Here the victories have been won in the press, in the legislative halls, and in courts of law. Working with men, or alone, they have perfected organisation, agitated, raised money, printed appeals, and carried cases through the courts, until factories and stores have been made safer, excessive working hours have been cut down, young children have been exempted from labour, many sweat-shops have been closed, and women workers have begun to be organised to care for their own needs. Much has been done; more remains to be done; but the training of the women has gone steadily forward.

These, then, are the forces which have pushed women forward in America: European political and religious persecution, the forest necessities of colonial life, the American Revolution, the struggle with slavery and intemperance, the Civil War, the industrial struggle and the need to protect women and children from capitalistic exploitation. Possibly women have now reached a point in their development where they can turn to public service and to a full realisation of their powers and responsibilities without the goading necessity of a great wrong. If not, there are sufficient wrongs still calling to lead them for many years. Intemperance is not yet banished; the negro is not yet freed from the effects of his slavery; working women and children are not yet fairly protected; disease reaps needlessly large harvests; Lazarus still begs at the table of Dives; our public education leaves much to be desired; criminals are badly handled; millions of European refugees come marching into our land needing guidance. Meantime, millions of women are content, because themselves comfortable, and there are some even willing to aid the powers of obstruction.

In these later years, marvellous changes have taken place all over the world. Even in China, official attempts are now being made to leave women free to walk by abolishing the bandaging of infants' feet. In Turkey, women are going out from the harem to participate in public life. In Germany, they are escaping from the exclusive service of the home. In England, they are repeating the cries of the men of 1776 and of 1789: "All men and women are born free and equal." "No taxation without representation." "One person, one vote." In Finland, Australia, New Zealand, Norway and Sweden, women have all the essential civic and political rights of men.

But, as in all human progress, first the ideas of a few leaders change; they shape legislation; and the new organisation slowly makes over the practices and then the deep-seated mental and moral habits, which constitute popular prejudices. These old unreasoning feelings still largely dominate us, blinding us to the facts of life and blocking each new advance by which women might pass into the world of free choice and adjustment of their lives as co-workers with men. In the next chapters we must study these present-day conditions in detail.

Women in Education

N DISCUSSING WOMAN'S relation to formal education we are really examining her ability to master and teach certain intellectual exercises, for in our modern industrial democracies our efforts are confined almost exclusively to training the mind and to stocking it with information. Each year we talk more and more about physical, moral, political, social and industrial education; but requirements for entrance into schools, promotions in them, and graduation from their courses, still rest almost entirely on information acquired; and in a less degree, on intellectual ability displayed.

Even in selecting and certifying teachers, the emphasis is all laid on intellectual equipment. On the physical, moral, or social sides we at most demand that the candidates shall not be too bad; on the political side we do not demand even this, since nearly 80 per cent. of our whole teaching force is declared legally unfit to vote or hold office, and is yet employed to train our future citizens. But on the intellectual side we demand positive proof of fitness. Thus it is fair to say that our modern education deals almost exclusively with knowledge.

Knowledge, in the past, has nearly always been considered much as we consider dynamite today. It was a dangerous force, useful to a ruling class, and hence preserved in the hands of a cult, generally a priesthood; but it was thought capable of working endless mischief in the hands of ignorant people. Through all the pages of history we find individuals, and weaker groups, driven away from the accumulated treasure; and if detected in their desire to know, especially if they sought knowledge through original investigation, they were branded with such titles of disgrace as "wizard" or "heretic;" and, as a warning to others, they were often burned in the public square or buried alive.

Women, as an inferior class, were especially restrained from learning. Knowledge would breed discontent in them; it would make them question the binding power of the conventions and beliefs which held them in their place; and it would show them how to achieve their freedom, and might even encourage them to assume leadership Here and there, individual women gained the training necessary for leadership, as in the cases of Sappho, Aspasia or Hypatia; but the great mass of women was sternly repressed. Eve leads a long line of women martyrs who, across the ages, have paid a great price for their desire to eat of the tree of knowledge. For herself, she might have paid the price but, with subtle understanding of women, the penalty was made to involve all whom they loved; the terrors of that price have held the sex in restraint ever since. Eurydice, Pandora, Eve, Lot's wife and Bluebeard's wife have in turn served as awful warnings. After a time it came to be understood by women that they should fix their eyes on their husbands and never look forward or backward, lest they lose their Eden and drag those whom they loved after them to destruction.

Of course, if women could not learn they could not teach; at least, they could not teach where it was necessary to impart knowledge; and so their share in formal education has been slight, until our own time. Young children have been considered their special charge, and the care and culture of infancy and young childhood have always rested in the hands of mothers, grandmothers, aunts and female servants. Beyond these early years, however, woman's part has been restricted to emphasising, mainly with girls, the dogmas and practices of caste, kitchen and church.

These were the conditions which prevailed through early Oriental and Classical times. Christianity brought women some degree of intellectual freedom, but it also imposed new forms of restraint. Its fundamental teachings, based as they were on a belief in individual values, were favourable to the extension of knowledge and to the opening of opportunity for all. The Church, however, shaped under the half-civilised conditions of the Middle Ages, quickly took knowledge into her own keeping, forbade its extension, and increasingly held before woman, as her highest ideal, the negative virtues of the cloister.

The humanistic and theological changes which came with the awakening of the European mind at the close of the Middle Ages, did much to set free the accumulated treasures of knowledge. Protestantism, by exalting individual judgement and insisting on the necessity of each one reading and judging the sacred records for himself, made it possible for even women to enter into the heritage of the ages. At least, the key to learning, reading, was given into her hands. Later Protestant sects broke down the limits of sacerdotalism, until women found that they could look forward a little way without losing their Edens, or could even glance backward without being turned into pillars of reproach.

The political revolutions of the eighteenth century also affirmed in their point of view the same intellectual freedom for women as for men. It has taken a long time to make the practical adjustments, but they are now well under way. Since 1870, women have had very great freedom in their approach to knowledge; and having knowledge, they have been allowed to impart it to others.

In America, freedom for women to study has moved more rapidly than in Europe. Even in the colonial period, there were emancipated women, as we have seen; and in the last half of the eighteenth century several schools were opened for girls, which were more than polite finishing schools. Notable among these institutions were the seminary at Bethlehem, Pa, opened in 1753 by the Moravians, and the school established by the Society of Friends, in Providence, RI, in 1784. But nearly all girl's schools before 1800 were limited to terms of a few months, where girls attended to learn needle-work, music and dancing, and to cultivate their morals and manners.

At the close of the Revolutionary War, the leaders of public opinion universally recognised that their new experiment in government would succeed only if the voters were intelligent.

This statement of belief became the major premise on which all arguments for free and compulsory education were based; and while we have practically accepted a much wider justification for education, in connection with the care of defectives, industrial training, and other recent movements, we have not yet changed our formulated philosophy concerning the relation of the state to its children. Free and compulsory education is still mainly justified on the ground that it produced good citizens.

But the women had not full citizenship and hence the argument for general education did not apply to them. Had they been enfranchised after the Revolution, all educational opportunities would have been open to them at once as a matter of course; and an immense amount of struggle, futile effort, and unnecessary friction would have been saved. But this larger view of woman's rights and powers would have required an adjustment in deep-seated ideas and prejudices, concerning her proper position, too great to be undertaken by men facing a new form of government and the material problems of a new world.

But even without this change in ideas, economic conditions steadily forced the women into educational activity. There were not enough men available to teach the scattered country schools, and citizens had to be trained for the needs of the new democracy. John Adams recognised this when he wrote to Mr Warren that their wives must "teach their sons the divine science of politics;" though he would have been one of the last to favour admitting women to full participation in public life. He did not realise that if women were to train men for citizenship, the rudiments of knowledge which they had learned in scattered schools and in their poor little academies must be greatly supplemented. Life, however, is never logical, and at this advance men balked. Necessity was forcing women into schools as teachers, and hence into larger preparation for their own lives; but public opinion, here as elsewhere, failed to recognise the forces that were compelling its action.

Thus the work of furnishing more advanced intellectual training for American women had to be started by the women themselves. This is possibly the first time in human history that a great group of people feeling itself irresistibly moving toward a social, industrial and political readjustment, little less than revolutionary in its nature, has gone deliberately to work to prepare for the change through education. The working classes of the world are doing the same thing now; but women showed them the way. In some vague degree, American women recognised the truth which Dr. Gore recently brought before a mass of working men in England. "All this passion for justice will accomplish nothing," he declared, "unless you get knowledge. You may become strong and clamorous, you may win a victory, you may affect a revolution, but you will be trodden down again under the feet of knowledge if you leave knowledge in the hands of privilege, because knowledge will always win over ignorance."**21**

American women were fortunate, too, in having for their leaders such women as Emma Willard, Mary Lyon and Catherine Beecher. Emma Willard was a woman of the world; she had travelled abroad and she brought to her work a cultivated nature, wide experience of life and natural leadership Her personality went far toward lifting the movement to a plane of respect. After trying a little academy in Vermont, she appealed to the State of New York in 1814 for help In this appeal, she wisely adopted the prevailing view of the relation of the state to education. The state must have good citizens, she repeats, and then goes on, "The character of children will be formed by their mothers; and it is through the mothers that the government can control the character of its future citizens." The State of New York granted her articles of incorporation for her academy at Waterford, NY, but refused her the modest sum of five thousand dollars for which she had asked. In 1821, she established the Troy Female Seminary, where for years she trained and led the intellectual life of American women.

Miss Mary Lyon begged the money from the common people with which she opened Mount Holyoke Seminary in 1837. Those who feared the education of women were disarmed by the fact that in the new institution domestic service was emphasised to the extent of having the girls do all their own work. Another group of possible critics was won over by the fact that religious instruction received constant care. But notwithstanding the conserving influence of housework and religion, there went steadily out from Mount Holyoke during the following years a strong line of teachers demanding ever larger opportunity for themselves and for those they taught.

Miss Catherine Beecher added to her work in schools for girls a general propaganda for woman's education, and she devised large plans for its development. In 1852, she organised the American Woman's Educational Association "to aid in securing to American women a liberal education, honourable position, and remunerative employment." She helped to start girls' schools in half a dozen cities, and by writing and talking she sowed in the hearts of women, especially in the Middle West, a discontent with existing conditions and a deep desire to know.

From the time of this awakening in the thirties and forties, two lines of educational activity for the advancement of woman's education steadily developed. One was the effort of women to educate themselves in distinctly women's schools; and the other was the movement by which existing institutions for boys and men were gradually opened to girls and women. These two lines of activity still remain distinct, and not always sympathetic with each other's aims.

The effort to establish distinctly women's schools was continued after the Civil War by Matthew Vassar, who founded in 1861, and opened in 1865, the first adequately endowed and organised college for women in America. Ten years later, Miss Sophie Smith founded and endowed Smith College to furnish women "with means and facilities for education equal to those that are offered in colleges for young men." The institution was opened in 1875; and in the same year Henry Durant established Wellesley College.

The last Report of the United States Commissioner of Education shows that there are now 108 institutions of higher learning to which men are not admitted; but most of them have modelled themselves so closely upon men's colleges that they have not been able to work out lines of distinctive instruction specially fitted to women. One cannot help feeling that since they do not open their doors to men they should do something more toward working out an ideal education for women than they have so far undertaken. When the Association of Intercollegiate Alumnae met in New York, in the autumn of 1911, its discussions gathered around the possibility of adding to college courses subjects of special value to women. Hygiene, biology and sociology were the subjects most favoured; but the matter needs attention from women and men who stand outside the group dominated by our older college traditions. This movement to provide distinctive schools for women had brought together, in 1910, 35,714 girl students in private secondary schools and 9,082 women students in higher institutions of learning.

The second line of development, which sought to open up all existing schools to girls and women, began when Boston opened a high school for girls in 1825. New York opened a high school for girls three years later.

It was in the West, however, that this movement took strongest root and made most steady advance. The West has always led the East in opening equal opportunity to women, even equal suffrage. The forest and the frontier compel such action even in such commonwealths as Australia, New Zealand and Canada, where there has been no political revolution to hasten it. Labour is scarce; the invading people are intelligent and ambitious for their children and desire them educated. The women must teach them to read and write; the girls learn with their brothers; and so the women master the mysteries of formal education.

Thus it is no accident that Oberlin, in the western forest, was the first college to open its doors to women. Antioch, under Horace Mann's direction, was, however, the first institution of higher learning to give men and women equal opportunity. The new States of the Mississippi Valley early established State universities. These institutions were little more than seminaries, but the free spirit of the frontier was so strong in them that in 1863 Wisconsin University admitted women to its privileges, and Kansas and

Indiana followed shortly after.

It is the year 1870, however, that marks the beginning of a new period in the higher education of women as in so many other lines of advance. In that year, Michigan University, California University and the University of Evanston, adopted co-education. Michigan was just entering on a great career and her influence was very important. There, for the first time, women could follow a university curriculum under the same conditions as men. Two years later, Andrew D. White introduced the Michigan idea at Cornell.

In the forty years since Michigan opened her doors, the advance of women under conditions of co-education has been steady and rapid. In Harvard and Columbia opportunity takes the form of annexes where women can secure almost any educational opportunities they desire. In other universities, like Pennsylvania and Johns Hopkins, women are admitted to graduate study. Most of the institutions of higher education that do not yet admit women are theological and technical schools, or small colleges like Haverford, where there are equivalents in Swarthmore and Bryn Mawr, for women who wish to attend a Friend's College. A woman can work in almost any important university in America today if she cares to do so. In 1910 there were conferred in the United States 12,590 AB degrees, and women took 44.1 per cent of them.

Meantime, there have been no important reactions in institutions which have once opened their doors to women.**22** In 1902, Chicago University separated men and women students, but only during the first two years of their undergraduate work. Practically this has affected only one-half of the women in the first year and a very much smaller proportion in the second year.**23** When Leland Stanford Junior University was opened in 1891, 25.4 per cent of the students were women. This proportion rose in successive years as follows: 1892, 29.7 per cent; 1893, 30.4 per cent; 1894, 33.8 per cent; 1895, 35.3 per cent; 1896, 36.6 per cent; 1897, 37.4 per cent; 1898, 40.1 per cent. Fearing that the institution would be swamped with women, and that able men students would stay away, Mrs Stanford ruled that there should never be more than five hundred women students in the university at one time. This limit was reached in 1902, and it was then provided that women should not be received as special students, nor in partial standing. Later, men in partial standing were cut out, though they continued to be received as special students. Women are now admitted in order of application, but preference is given to juniors and seniors. This really establishes a higher standard for women than for men, and one would expect that men would be kept away from an institution requiring a higher standard for women quite as much as from one where there were many women working on an equality with men. In 1910, Tufts College decided to separate men and women, for local reasons. The statement was made at the time that a philanthropist had promised a gift of $500,000 for a woman's college, if the sexes were separated.**24** The doors of Wesleyan are to be closed to women after 1912, but this is due to local and financial reasons.

The movement in European universities, while not so uniform as in America, has been in the same direction. Miss Buss, Miss Beal and Miss Emily Sheriff led an early movement for higher secondary education of girls similar to that which gathered around Miss Willard in America. In 1871, Miss Clough started in England the lectures for women which led to the establishment of Newnham and Girton at Cambridge, and opened Oxford to women. Now women can study almost any subject they like at these universities and take the same examinations as the men. They do not receive degrees, but they have most of the other advantages of men, and for forty years they have carried off many honours. In the newer universities of London, Manchester, Leeds, Liverpool and in the Welsh University they have every advantage open to men.

In Germany, the opportunities for higher education of women have changed from year to year; but in 1910, there were 1,856 women in the universities as compared with 1,108 in 1909, and this notwithstanding the Emperor's well known belief that woman's sphere should be limited to domestic activities.

The claims advanced in opposition to the higher education of women have largely broken down today. It was long maintained that her mind was inferior to man's mind in kind and quality, and that she could not do the work required. In the presence of thousands of young women carrying all kinds of university work with credit and honour such charges become absurd. The belief that woman's health could not stand the strain fails for the same reason. The fear that she would be less likely to marry; or marrying, would be less likely to have children, has been seen to have some body of fact behind it; but we have seen also that university students are recruited from groups that are not the most fecund, and that the same danger applies to men students as to women.**25** Women in higher education are now accepted as a regular part of our modern life.

And yet there is one objection that still remains unanswered in very many minds. It has always been feared that women would lower the standard of scholarship; and there is much in the quality of the present generation of women students that may strengthen this belief. In the seventies and eighties, the fear of being thought peculiar still kept many ordinary women away from colleges. Now it has become fashionable, and a woman who has been to college stands better in a community than one who has not. Add to this the freedom and romance of "going to college" and it follows that many young women, with increasing economic freedom, are tempted to go up to the universities just as well-placed young Englishmen go to Cambridge or Oxford as passmen. They have no special interest in scholarship; but they like the life. This large body of young women, and of men under similar conditions, will doubtless lower the scholarship of modern college and university life as a whole. But possibly the need of the world for all-around men and women is even greater than its need for scholars; and in that case we may find justification for both passmen and passwomen.

With the opening of knowledge to women it became possible for them to instruct children in matters intellectual; and since our school learning was almost entirely a matter of information and mental training, they early became an important part of the teaching profession in America.

Once started, all our conditions favoured the rapid increase of women teachers. There were industrial openings for men on every side; and with our rapid increase in population, an army of teachers was required. Since the calling had in the past been filled by inferior members of the clergy, broken-down soldiers, or old women, there was a tradition of constant change, and young men on their way to permanent professions were steadily supplanted by young women on their way to the altar.

Co-education very materially assisted this substitution. Social, religious and economic reasons early combined to establish co-education in elementary schools in America, and now it has become a national custom. In cities like Philadelphia and Brooklyn there are some separate schools; but in 1910, only 4 per cent of all the elementary children and only 5 per cent of the children in public high schools were in separate classes. In private schools, which care for less than 10 per cent of the children of the country, the percentage of children in separate schools is greater.

Practically all American children are now in co-educational institutions. Had the boys been in schools by themselves it would have been more difficult to place women teachers over them, but in mixed schools the question does not arise. Even where the boys and girls were separated, however, that fact did not prevent the employment of women teachers, though it may have retarded it. Thus in Philadelphia, in 1911, there were 125 boys' classes, 174 girls' classes, and 894 mixed classes in the grammar grades; still there were but 175 men teachers employed and, of course, the girls' classes were all taught by women.

While administrative positions are less monopolised by women than teaching posts, they are being steadily filled by them. For fifteen years Idaho has had able women State superintendents elected by popular suffrage; Colorado and Montana have also given this highest educational post to women. In most of our States we have women serving as county superintendents; and in Idaho women fill nearly all these positions. Several of our largest cities, notably Chicago and Cleveland, have women superintendents;

while many high schools and most of our elementary schools have women principals. In 1909, Mrs Ella Flagg Young was elected president of the National Education Association; and in 1911, Miss Alice Dilley was elected president of the Iowa State Teachers' Association. Both of these elections were victories for women won in the face of determined opposition from many of the men.

Another feature of this monopoly of teaching by women should be emphasised. Many boards of education require a woman to resign her position if she marries, and married women are seldom appointed to teaching positions, except where they are widows or separated from their husbands. In a test case recently carried to the Supreme Court of the State of New York a decision was rendered that the Board of Education of New York City could not dismiss teachers for marrying; but by refusing leave of absence to prospective mothers the Board is still able to remove all women who dare to have children. Thus we have a modern industrial democracy being educated almost entirely by celibate women.

But why should a woman be forced to leave teaching because she marries? Would not married women do much to strengthen and broaden the calling? Are not married women better fitted than celibates to deal with boys and girls in the period of adolescence? There is doubtless a feeling that a married woman should make way for some girl who needs the position to help herself along; but schools should not be used for the needs of teachers, no matter how deserving the individual may be.

There is, too, a possibility that a married woman might have a child, and a feeling that this would shock the other teachers and the children. Surely we have grown beyond this condition; the teacher could easily be given a leave of absence for a few months, or for a few years; and nowhere else could the children better meet this fact of universal existence around which our Anglo-Saxon reticence has woven such a shameful conspiracy of silence. At least, when a woman has passed the period of childbearing she could bring to the school incalculable gifts of balanced judgement and ripe understanding of life.

Meantime all the influences which have brought about the

monopoly of teaching by women are increasingly operative. Every year more able women leave our high schools, normal schools and universities, with no corresponding new lines of occupation open to them. The feeling of rivalry between men and women teachers grows stronger each year. Powerful teachers' federations, such as those in Chicago and Buffalo, composed mainly of women, are said to be using their influence to favour women. In New York City, the women teachers have compelled the city to equalise the wages of men and women, at an annual expense of $3,500,000, after a bitter fight lasting several years.

The effects of this monopoly upon the women themselves are very difficult to estimate. Some alarmists tell us that women teachers face the danger of a premature and loveless old age; that the celibate communities they form in the commonwealth are marked by pettiness and emotionalism; that the salaries paid teachers are so small that they cannot provide for sickness and old age, and that, unless pensioned by the state, some of them must one day eat the bread of charity.

On the other hand, we are told that education is the natural province of women; that teaching fits them to be good mothers and helpful citizens; that women alone can form the character of girls; and that boys are refined and perfected by the constant contact with women.

Probably neither of these statements is wholly true. It is certain that many women teachers do marry, do become the mothers of fine children, and are social forces in their communities. With advancing standards of scholarship, better salaries, old age pensions, and a popular demand for professional efficiency in teachers, it will be increasingly difficult for men to use the calling as a preparation for law and medicine, or for women to use it as a preparation for matrimony. The calling doubtless does offer a greater equivalent for marriage than most others; and many women live their mother life vicariously for other people's children.

At the same time, however, when a woman has given fourteen years of her life to preparation for teaching, eight years in an elementary school, four in a high school, and from two to four in professional training, she has made an investment and formed habits which will make her hesitate before turning to matrimony. The independence and income will prove attractive during young maidenhood; and matrimony can hardly yield its best results to the woman who enters it after she is thirty. It is certainly true that women are decreasingly willing to enter the teaching profession; and in many parts of the country there is a chronic dearth of trained teachers.

Meantime, for good or ill, women have eaten, and are eating of the tree of knowledge as they will. If this has driven them out of the little paradise of the past, they are in a fair way to make the whole world into a paradise of the present. Only through training their minds could they have broken away from an outworn past. In this time of readjustment there must be many mistakes and many tragedies.**26** The fool-killer will gather a rich harvest, but if we are open-minded and eager to see the truth, each martyr will teach her sisters, and the future generations of women will conserve the values of the past and add to them new treasures and new graces of knowledge and understanding.

It is most unfortunate that these real issues should be obscured by sex rivalry. There can be no real rivalry between a man's soul and his body, between science and religion, between man and woman. Such antagonisms rest back in the failure to realise the incompleteness of man or woman alone, for any purposes of life. And there is, too, that evil notion which still affects economics, that when two trade one must lose. The fact is that in all honest exchange buyer and seller gain alike, and all who participate become rich. It is so in all honest relations between these half-creatures we call men and women. In agreement, association, cooperation, lies strongest significant life for both. In separation, competition and antagonism lie arid, poor, mean lives, conceited and egotistic, vapid and contemptible.

The Feminising of Culture

ITH THE WEAKENING of sex prejudices and the removal of legal restrictions on women's freedom it was inevitable that they should invade fields of activity where formerly only men were found. Since women must eat every one knew that they must work, and the sight of a woman at work was no new experience. Even in the days when they were most secluded and protected, the number kept in ease was always very small compared with the women slaves and servants who spun, cooked and served. Hence men were used to seeing women at work; and while industrial adjustments have not been easily made, they have still been accepted as a matter of course. But who, fifty years ago, could have imagined that today women would be steadily monopolising learning, teaching, literature, the fine arts, music, the church and the theatre? And yet that is the condition at which we have arrived. We may scoff at the way women are doing the work, and reject the product, but that does not alter the fact that step by step women are taking over the field of liberal culture as opposed to the field of immediately productive work.

Some of the reasons for this change are so clear that it seems as though they might have been anticipated. In a comparatively few years the greater part of Western Europe and all of America has become rich, not this time through the enslavement of other peoples and the confiscating of their wealth, but through the enslaving and exploitation of the material forces of nature. This wealth is not well distributed, but large numbers of families have received enough so that the women do not have to work constantly with their hands. At this point all historic precedent would have turned these women into luxury-loving parasites and playthings.

A good many of them have taken this easiest way and entered the peripatetic harems of the rich. But several million women refused to repeat the old cycle of ruin; they knew too much.**27** What then should they do? Faith in the value of conventual life for women had passed; industrial changes had transformed their homes so that the endless spinning, weaving, sewing and knitting were no longer there, even to be supervised. Penelope's tasks had passed to foremen, working under trades union agreements, in the factories of Fall River and Birmingham. Even the function of the lady bountiful who looked after the spiritual and family affairs of her tenants and servants and distributed doles and Christmas baskets was gone. Her tenants owned their own farms, and her chauffeur resented her interference with his personal life. What should she do?

And this movement was not confined to the rich, for those who were not yet economically free were still deeply influenced by the changes which were taking place. The Goulds, Stanfords, Vanderbilts, Floods, Carnegies and Schwabs had all been lifted from the level of the masses to financial grandeur before the eyes of the multitude, and democratic ambitions drove parents who thought themselves in the line of financial advancement to secure culture for their girls in time. If the daughter was destined to live on Fifth Avenue, or to marry a duke, it was best to get her ready while young. In all our industrial democracies, armies of American parents have devoted themselves to labour, and even sacrificed comforts and necessities, that the daughters might get ready to live easier and fuller lives than the parents had known. If the choice had to be made between the girl and her brother, the chivalry of the father and the ambition of the mother very often gave the opportunity to the girl.

And so an emancipated army of leisure has been formed which has transformed the very nature of the culture with which it has busied itself. Books, periodicals, musical instruments, travel became cheaper and cheaper as the demand increased. Wholesale production makes almost any luxury accessible to every one. It is also possible to find modern and agreeable forms for older academic exercises. If Greek and Latin were too full or too difficult, courses in Romanic and Germanic philology would do as well. Anglo-Saxon gave way to Old English; and Chaucer to the Lake Poets. Philosophy struggled for favour with the English novel on equal terms. The works of Raphael were photographed and lithographed until the Sistine Madonna became as commonly known as the face of any strenuous and popular statesman of the day. With the aid of these art productions, and John Addington Symonds, every woman with leisure became an art critic. If economics was not interesting, sociology was available; and it could be democratised to any degree desired. If travel was troublesome, one could leave it to Cook; buy a ticket and he would do the rest.

If these awakening hungers and corresponding opportunities had affected only the period of life formerly thought available for education, these changes would have come about much more slowly than they have. But the genetic conception of life, steadily popularised since 1870, has led us to see that education is coterminous with life. It seems strange that we should have ever thought that mental activity belongs alone to youth. Dorland's study shows that in a list of four hundred fairly representative great men, only 10.25 per cent ceased their mental activity between the ages of forty and fifty; 20.75 per cent between fifty and sixty; 35 per cent between sixty and seventy; 22.5 per cent between seventy and eighty; and 6 per cent after eighty.**28**

The recognition of such facts as these has given us a new genetic sense of life, under the influence of which mothers and grandmothers have joined the younger women in the pursuit of culture. They have formed clubs — study clubs, current events clubs, camera clubs, art clubs, literary clubs, civic clubs. They have organised courses of university extension lectures; enrolled in Chicago University correspondence courses; and have flocked to Chautauqua by the thousand in the summer, when not abroad. It is not through the generosity of men that liberal culture has come into the possession of women; they have carried it by storm and have compelled capitulation.

Judging by the facts presented in the last chapter, women are pretty fully in possession of formal education. If we examine this monopoly a little more carefully, we shall find that while in the kindergarten and in the elementary schools boys furnish 51 per cent of the enrolment, simply because more boys are born in civilised communities than girls, as soon as we reach the high schools, girls increasingly take the lead. In 1910, the girls formed 56.45 per cent of the enrolment in high schools — or there were 110,249 more girls than boys. The proportion of girls increased through each of the four years of the course, and of the graduates, 60.8 per cent were girls. In the public normal schools, 64.45 per cent of the students were girls.

The universities, colleges and technical schools, which are massed together in our government reports, had hardly any women students in 1870; in 1880, 19.3 per cent of the students were women; in 1890, 27 per cent; in 1910, 30.4 per cent. In all these institutions we had enrolled in 1910, 17,707 women. Of 602 institutions reported in 1910, 142 were for men only; 108 were for women only; and 352 were open to both sexes. But here again the influence of women increases during each of the four years for, as we have seen, the women took 41.1 per cent of the A.B. degrees granted in 1910. It is surely not too much to say that, if present conditions continue, women will soon be in an overwhelming majority in all secondary and higher education in the United States.

If we examine the teaching force, we find this monopoly already established. In 1870, when our government records begin, 59 per cent of the teachers were women; in 1880, 57.2 per cent were women; in 1890, 65.5 per cent; in 1900, 70.1 per cent; in 1910, 78.6 per cent. The more settled and intelligent the community the more rapid this advance has been. Thus Arkansas has 52.4 per cent women teachers; but Massachusetts has 91.1 per cent and Connecticut has 93 per cent.

In cities, too, the women fill nearly all teaching positions. New York City has 89 per cent women in its force; Boston, 89 per cent; Philadelphia, 91.4 per cent; Chicago, 93.3 per cent. In many cities the proportion is even greater than this: Omaha has 97 per cent; Wheeling, W Va, 97.5 per cent; Charleston, SC, 99.3 per cent; and in forty-six American towns of 4,000 to 8,000 inhabitants there is no man teaching. When we remember that many of the men indicated above are in high schools or in supervising posts, we are prepared for the statement in a report recently laid before the Board of Education of New York City that in half the cities of the United States there are virtually no men teaching.

In our high schools, 54 per cent of the teachers are women; in public normal schools, 65 per cent; and in institutions of higher learning 17.6 per cent are women. Even in supervising positions, there are more women than men in the large centres of population. Certainly these figures justify us in saying that women have established a monopoly of education in the United States, except in the higher institutions.

In order to discuss the effects which this monopoly of education by women is having on the curriculum of the schools we must first agree on what constitutes the peculiarity of women's minds as compared with men's minds.**29** In our first chapter, it was asserted that women are more interested in the concrete, human, personal, conserving and emotional aspects of life; while men more easily turn to the abstract, material, impersonal, creative and rational aspects. To put it broadly, women are more interested in the humanities; men more readily pursue the sciences. Let us admit at once that there are many individual exceptions to this statement. Some women have reached great excellence in abstract studies; and some men are notoriously concrete and emotional; but nevertheless the general statement seems borne out by a wealth of common observations and detailed comparisons.

Personal observation must always be coloured by prejudices and prepossessions, but my own have been so wide, and so uniformly in one direction, that it seems justifiable to report them. quarter of a century I have been working in schools or with teachers, and my personal observations all agree with the above characterisation. I have spent five years in Cornell University,

New York; one year in Zurich University in Switzerland; two years in the State University of Indiana and seven years in Stanford University in California. These institutions are widely distributed; they were all fully co-educational; and they each had a wide range of elective studies. In all of them, classrooms devoted to literature and modern languages had a large attendance of women, while lecture-rooms and laboratories devoted to abstract science were almost deserted by them. This could not have been due to commercial considerations, for many of these women were facing teaching; and during all this time the demand for women who could teach science has been much greater than for women who could teach literature.

In my work with teachers, both in the classroom and in the field, I have carried out many inductive, quantitative studies, based on measurements or returns from large numbers of children. I have never found women teachers taking up and carrying out this kind of work with any such enthusiasm as men apply to it, though it lies at the base of their professional life.

Institutional generalisations seem all to point in this same direction. For instance, the Girls' Evening High School in Philadelphia is managed by one of the best known scientific women in the country, Dr L L W Wilson, head of the biological department of the Philadelphia Normal School. With a thousand girls of high school grade, under the leadership of a scientific woman, the only science courses given in the school are those in domestic science. The reason is that the girls, most of them not being candidates for a degree, will not take up science work, though they form strong classes in literature and languages.

If, from such general facts of observation, one turns to exact comparisons, where quantities can be measured, the results are all the same. Of students enrolled in classical departments of universities, colleges and technical schools reporting to the United States Bureau of Education, in 1910, 36.5 per cent were women, while of those enrolled in general science courses, but 17.2 per cent were women. In 1,511 public and private high schools and seminaries, reporting to the Bureau of Education in 1909-1910, a larger percentage of boys than of girls was enrolled in algebra, geometry, trigonometry, physics, chemistry, physical geography, civil government and rhetoric, which is a scientific study of language. A larger proportion of girls enrolled in Latin, French, German, English literature and history, and there was a slightly greater enrolment of girls in botany, zoology and physiology.

In the further discussion of this subject it will then be taken for granted that in education, feminisation means emphasis on languages, literature and history, as opposed to mathematics, physics, chemistry and civics. For the elementary schools we have no data capable of reduction to figures, but general observation, backed by an examination of courses of study and textbooks, will compel any one to say that in twenty years we have made wonderful progress in reading, language, stories, mythology, biography and history; while all our efforts to bring nature work into vital relation with the schools have borne little fruit. Our country schools need lessons in agriculture, and the children should gain a deep sense of country life. But how can celibate young women, longing toward the towns, give this? Any subjects well taught are sure to be increasingly taught, and it takes no extended study to see that our elementary schools are being feminised in the direction of literature. This is the more striking when we remember that these twenty years have been dominated, in the larger world, by scientific interests.

In the high schools and seminaries, we have fairly complete returns showing the number of students enrolled in certain subjects since 1890. The pupils taking Latin have increased 15 per cent; French, 4 per cent; German, 13 per cent; English literature has increased in ten years 7 per cent (there is no record for this subject before 1898); and European history, 27 per cent. There has also been an increase of 11 per cent in algebra and 10 per cent in geometry, probably partly due to vocational need and to the emphasis laid on these subjects for admission to college. But physics, in the twenty years under consideration, has fallen off 7 per cent; chemistry, 3 per cent; physical geography, 5 per cent; physiology, 15 per cent; and civics, 7 per cent.**30** A careful study of these figures must convince any fair-minded person that our school curriculum, even in the secondary field, where women's control is least complete, is moving rapidly in the direction of what we have called feminisation.

The schools, too, must increasingly do something more than train the intellect; and in all physical activity involuntary suggestion is very powerful. Playgrounds are laboratories of conduct, and they should not only give physical exercise, but should also furnish standards and ideals. There can be no doubt that women are physically more restrained, retiring, non-contesting, and graceful than men; but can dancing, marching, and gymnastics take the place of more aggressive, direct and violent contests in the training of boys? So in industries, women are more given to conserving, arranging and beautifying, more given to clerking and recording, while men are more creative, disbursing, more given to mining, agriculture and commerce. Even granting equal understanding and experience, the tradition of the race must count for much; and it would seem that at every stage of growth, boys and girls alike should feel the impulse to imitate men who have an instinct to make and unmake, to trade and carry. It is no justification of existing conditions to say that the men now in the teaching profession lack these qualities; if they do, let us get rid of them and have real men. And for purposes of political life, does it not seem strange to bring up a generation of boys and girls who are to be the future citizens of a democracy under the exclusive leadership of people who have never been encouraged to think about political life nor allowed to participate in it? Let us by all means enfranchise women; but even then they cannot hope to quickly catch up with those who have some thousands of years the start, even after allowing for the fact that girls inherit from both father and mother.

Most of these differences which we have been discussing seem to rest in the fact that women are more personal in their interests and judgements than men are. This may be due to their education for thousands of years; but that makes it no less true. Women certainly, in a great majority of cases, are more interested in a case than in a constitution; in a man than in a mission; in a poem that in a treatise; in equity than in law. In a generation when everything is tending toward great aggregations, consolidated industries, segregated wealth, and new syntheses of knowledge, both boys and girls should have such training as will fit them to play their part in these larger units.

As to the feminising influence of exclusively women teachers on manners and morals and general attitude toward life there can be no real doubt. Boys and girls cannot spend eight or twelve impressionable years of childhood and youth under the constant daily influence of women without having the ladylike attitude toward life strongly emphasised. To deny this is to repudiate the power of constant involuntary suggestion and association. Whether it is desirable or not, is another question. The change may be all in the direction of advancing civilisation; but just as in the assimilation of our subject races, the philosophic mind must be distressed by the disappearance of so many varieties of speech, customs, and artistic and industrial products, so in this present assimilation, one cannot help regretting the steady disappearance of the katabolic qualities of the human male. One does not need to say that this feminised product is better or worse than what we have had, but it is certainly narrower, and less in harmony with the world's thought and work, than it formerly was.

If we turn from education to the press we have similar conditions. During these past few years, hundreds of journals have sprung up devoted to women's special interests. They are almost all of them showy, fragmentary, personal, concrete and emotional. It is difficult to find one that represents general or abstract interests. At least one of these journals which boasts a fabulous circulation is supported by its women subscribers and readers to oppose the larger interests of women in education, industry and political life. At least, if it does not oppose these interests, it does not aid them. Imagine a million German women sending the Kaiser one dollar and a half a year to induce him to tell them once a month to go back to their kitchens, churches and children!

The newspapers of America have steadily changed during the last three decades in the same direction. Editorial pages and news columns have been steadily modified in the direction of fragmentary, egoistic, personal and sensational, or at least emotional, appeals. These are the qualities of children's minds and of undeveloped minds everywhere. The change is, of course, a part of the larger democratic movement of our time, and many causes have contributed to bring it about. Had women not been so active, something of the same sort would have happened; but if women were all to forget how to read overnight, there is little doubt that the newspapers would find it advantageous to print more statesmanlike editorials and more general and abstract news.

With the weeklies and monthlies, the change taking place is the same. The new reading public, brought in by increase in population and by popular education, does not support the *Atlantic,* the *Century* and *Scribner's,* but turns to *Munsey's, McClure's* and *Everybody's*. The very change in names speaks of the new personal and egoistic element that has come into journalism. Of course, such changes are only in part due to the influence of women, but the change is in the direction of the qualities that characterise distinctively women's journals.

In books, the personal and romantic novel has taken precedence over every other form of literature. Many of these are written by women; their circulation, both through libraries and through sales, is much greater with women than with men; and in many of them the personal gossip is as transient as that which fills the evening papers.**31**

In the churches, especially in the ritualistic churches, women have long been the faithful attendants. Nowhere, except in the churches which make a rationalistic and abstract appeal, and in the Ethical Societies, does one find a preponderance of men. In 1903, a careful enumeration of all attendants at places of worship was made in the city of London. The count was taken on fair Sundays in autumn, and covered both morning and evening services. Sixty-one per cent of all adult attendants were women, 146,372 more women than men passing through the doors.

About the same time a similar census was made in the part of New York City lying on Manhattan Island. The women were in excess by 171,749, and formed 69 per cent of all attendants. Even church service, if not entirely tied to set forms, must seek to interest those who occupy the pews; and no observer can fail to note in both England and America, a movement toward ritualism on the one hand, and on the other, toward popular, personal, concrete and sometimes sensational preaching. The same general changes are taking place in libraries, in the drama, in concerts, in all group activities connected with learning and the fine arts.

But on the other side, if emancipated women had not applied themselves, since 1870, to the direction of education, literature, religion and amusements, all these interests must have suffered serious neglect and probable deterioration through the concentrating of the interests of the ablest men in engineering, manufacturing, commerce and other fields of pure and applied science. By popularising these interests, women have really humanised them, as all similar revolutions have done in the past. In breaking up old forms and intellectual conventions they have set free new and vital impulses. Whether the historian of the future will consider this period of democratisation and feminisation a time of advance may be uncertain; but it is certainly a time of liberated energy and of broadening participation in all that is best in life.

The Economic Independence of Women

OWHERE DOES A human being escape compulsion. Even were he alone in the world he would be forced to obey the physical laws governing gravity, heat, cold, hunger and disease. No matter what his desires might be, he would find himself limited and constrained by fixed laws, the inexorable penalties of which he could escape only by obedience. If the man were not alone, then each one of his companions would limit his freedom, and he would limit each one in the group, if they were to live together in peace and efficiency; and yet each of the man's companions would help to free him from the tyranny of physical forces, from the social pressure of others, and even from the bondage of his own nature.

Independence is thus an ideal to be achieved only through obedience. It begins in self-subordination and reaches its finest realisation in social subordination. Since the beginning of time men who thought have always dreamed of freedom; and for two hundred years now independence has been a word to conjure with. But in so far as independence means freedom to follow one's own unregulated desires, it is a fantastic and dangerous dream; and yet this dream of impossible independence has been among the greatest influences in furthering human development in the past.

The old-time dependence of one individual on the immediate caprices of another largely disappeared with the passing of slavery. But in place of this personal subjection has come a more complex and in some ways more compelling and crushing control through the monopoly of wealth. Property has become the medium through which the most binding of human relations are organised.

Accumulated wealth has become a great reservoir of power to which some individuals gain access through rights of birth, others through carefully guarded privileges, and still others through cunning devices or through force; but the masses of the people must gain their fragments of this wealth through arduous lifelong labour. Even the earth, the original source of all wealth, is parcelled out, and all of it is now owned by individuals or groups who control it in their own interests. One man may thus have thousands of acres which he cannot use, and which he will not allow others to use, while another has not where to lay his head. Laws jealously guard this wealth, which is the key to all opportunity; and public opinion, that most subtle, pervasive and compelling of all forms of law, gathers a thousand sacred initiations, rites, ceremonies, prohibitions and ex-communications around it. A man who has killed his neighbour, or ruined his friend's family, may be less punished by society than one who cheats at cards.

In primitive life a man may be a man by virtue of what he is; today he may have all the rights and privileges of any man by virtue of what he possesses. In any community can be found strong men, honest, though misplaced or unfortunate, begging bread, wasting their lives for want of money to live decently. And beside these one sees other men of weak physique and feeble minds, who have lived as parasites on society all their lives, but who are handsomely dressed, well fed, and possessed of power to do as they will, simply because they have access to wealth. It is no wonder that if one would seek freedom today in America he must look for her image on a gold coin.

It is not difficult to see why property has become such a powerful instrument in civilisation. Anything which a person really owns, in a psychological sense, is a home for his soul. Really owning an object, a toy, a garment, a watch or a home, means infusing one's personality into it. A man who possesses significant things has a new body through which his soul can work; this body trains his powers; and it should give him life more abundantly. A landless man must become a soulless man. Of course, we are not here speaking of legal ownership Many people own legally things into which they have never infused themselves; sometimes they have so many things that no individual could possibly infuse himself into them.

These conditions may prevail even in primitive life, but today they have been vastly increased through the fact that with advancing civilisation money was devised. This is a system of counters, generally coin or paper, not really valuable in themselves, but always resting back for value on the earth, or on something derived from it. In the past it was supposed that there were some things which, because of their nature, were not marketable, while others were beyond price. Today we set values on everything, even on men's bodies; eyes, ears, legs and lives can be priced. There are, in fact, insurance companies and factories that have regular schedules of value for various parts of the body. Our courts set prices on blighted affections, damaged reputations, social advancements, impaired digestions, damaged complexions, nervous shocks and extreme humiliations. Even a woman's honour may have a price in dollars.

These property rights, like the rights of the person, have always been subject to violence. Powerful individuals and groups have always been able to overstep legal restrictions and public opinion, and seize what they desired. The land grabbing going on in North Africa and Persia today and the activity of great industrial monopolies at home, show us that some property rights still need to be secured by force. In this struggle, it has come about naturally that men, being stronger, freer and less scrupulous than women, have outstripped them and have so far had a pretty complete monopoly of wealth. In fact women themselves have at times become property. In such times a man who stole or bought a woman, naturally took over with her all her rights in real estate and personal property as well as her person and her services.

Only gradually did women gain power to hold property themselves. Mainly because fathers wished to preserve property in their families, the right of women to inherit became slowly established as civilisation advanced. In Judea, Greece and Rome, certain rights of a woman to hold property were clearly settled. In the reversion to force under feudalism, woman's rights to outside property suffered; but they have been gradually restored during the last few centuries. Today, in civilised lands, a woman's rights to property, inherited or definitely given her or purchased by her, are everywhere recognised, if she does not marry. In France, and other Latin countries, she may still lose control of her property if she takes a husband; but in northern and western lands, even a married woman may retain her possessions.

Woman's body, too, is increasingly looked upon as her personal property. With the raising of the age of consent; with increasing severity in laws punishing rape, and with the abrogation of judicial orders for the restitution of marital rights, it is now quite generally recognised that a woman should have the right to control her own person. Still, in many lands there is much to be done before this right is fully safeguarded.

The place where a woman has not yet achieved economic freedom is in the disposal of her labour. One must remember, however, in this connection, that not only is there no fixed standard of values in human service as yet, but that many indispensable forms of service have not even been legally recognised as valuable. In early forms of civilisation, fighting and praying were considered the most important work the community received, and warriors and priests gained the big rewards. They received lands, gold, servants and dignities, while industrial workers, even the directors, were despised. Today we have reversed all this and we may pay a general only five thousand dollars a year, and a priest eight hundred dollars, while a man who develops a big industry may receive a hundred thousand dollars annually. Again, a man who invents a new gun may be given a fortune, like that of Herr Krupp, while a man who invents a surgical instrument is prevented by the ethics of his profession from even patenting it. If Pasteur had been paid for his services to France and to humanity, he would have ranked in the financial world with Mr Rockefeller and Mr Schwab. We pay a State superintendent of public instruction ten thousand dollars a year; but Miss Jane Addams, as instructor in ethics to the United States, receives no salary, and she must even beg the money to maintain her laboratory at Hull House. The whole question of payment for services is in a chaotic condition. Those who serve mankind most faithfully are rewarded on the principle, "From each according to his ability;" but nowhere is the remainder of the principle, "To each according to his needs," recognised. Hence our greatest servants must still beg support from our cleverest exploiters.

Domestic service is indispensable to society, but so far it has remained in the field of semi-slavery and uncertain barter; in a word, it is still in the feudal stage. The woman gives what she is and has, and nominally she gets protection and support. Sometimes these fail and, on the other hand, she occasionally receives the unearned gifts supposed to befit a potentate or a shrine. As women become educated they find this condition of uncertainty and instability unbearable. They are willing to work, but they must have a chance to think and to plan their lives according to their individual needs. Some degree of economic independence is necessary to intelligent thinking and orderly living. It is not that women are demanding more property; they are demanding some definite individual property as a home for their souls; and they are coming to realise that if this property rests on some one else's feelings and caprices it is no home for the soul; it is only a tavern.

This conception is well illustrated by the case of a woman in western New York, who married about 1850, and went to live on a farm with her husband. They had small means, but she brought seven hundred dollars to the altar, which was more than he possessed in ready capital. Her part was, however, soon swallowed up in the general business, and while there was a tacit agreement, voiced at long intervals, that she had put something into the business, her part never increased, though the man with whom she worked grew well-to-do. Certain feudal rights in the butter the woman made and in the chickens she raised, yielded her small sums, which often escaped her, but which she sometimes secured and put into a few silver spoons and dishes for her table, a square of Brussels carpet, three lace curtains, a marble topped stand, and six horsehair covered chairs for her parlour. These articles were considered in a very special sense her own. The man might have sold them and used the money, but public opinion would have condemned him had he done so.

Meantime the woman cooked for the family and the hired men, scrubbed and washed and mended. She strained and skimmed the milk from a dozen cows, and churned the butter; she fed the calves; cared for the hens; dug in the garden; gathered the vegetables; did the family sewing; and stole fragments of time for her flower-beds. Her hours were from five in the morning until nine at night, three hundred and sixty-five days in the year, with no half-days or Sundays off.

Incidentally she read her Bible, maintained religious exercises in the village, provided the church with a carpet by methods of indirection and kept the church clean. She upheld a moral standard toward which men only weakly struggled; hunted down and drove away all other women who refused equal service to their lords; ministered to the neighbouring sick; and doled out alms in winter-time. Her home was a social and industrial microcosm which she conducted as a feudal holding under the protection of her lord. It would be an interesting study to work out the rules of this feudal relation between husband and wife in any agricultural community. They would be found as varied, as unjust and arbitrary, and as generous, as those of the old régime in France.

A woman in a home is supposed to furnish three kinds of service. She must be a housekeeper, a wife and a mother. As housekeeper, her services can be estimated in current values running from three to twenty-five dollars a week with board and lodging. The other two kinds of service have never been reduced to monetary values.

As a wife, a woman is supposed to give her love, her person, her sympathy and inspiration; the personal care of a husband, including his clothes, attention to his relations and friends and general management of his social position and reputation. If she fills this position well, she is mistress, valet, confidential adviser and public entertainer. Possibly these services can be rated except the first, and even here the divorce courts scale alienated affections all the way from five hundred to twenty-five thousand dollars, according to the appearance of the woman and the skill of contending lawyers.

As a mother, the woman is supposed to give children a good heritage, nurse them, care for them, doctor them and train them. We have established values for these services as wet-nurse, nurse-maid, governess, doctor and teacher, but who can estimate a woman's value in giving a child a good heritage?

It is no wonder that such a difficult problem has remained thus far unsolved. Here and there a man gives his wife a household allowance, from the money they earn in common, and she struggles to save from it some fragments for her individual needs; others put their wives on a salary; and some others divide the income on a fractional basis. But the slightest study of existing conditions must convince any one that women are everywhere deeply dissatisfied with their economic relations to the family. On referring recently to this fact before an audience almost equally divided between suffragists and anti-suffragists, I found every woman present applauding the statement. Another time when I asked more than sixty of the wealthiest women in one of our cities how many were dissatisfied with their relations to the family property, explaining that I was not asking how many wanted more money but how many wanted a different relation to the family money, all the women raised their hands except three and they all had private property.

Meantime, economic changes, to be described in the next chapter, have transformed our homes and nearly eight million women have gone outside to earn money. The gladness with which they have gone shows that they were not afraid to work, though at first the money did not belong to them, but to their families. Almost everywhere in the United States the money women now earn is their own; only in Louisiana can the husband collect his wife's wages. Any one who reads Mrs. Gilman's masterly study of the evil effects accompanying woman's economic independence must feel how far-reaching are not only the discontent but also the evil influences of our present system through over-emphasising sex and through corrupting the public thinking and feeling concerning services and wages in general.**32**

Yet no one can seriously approach this problem in his own person without feeling that the relations of husband and wife contain elements that not only make it impossible to resolve the woman's service into money values, but that would make it useless to do so even if it could be done. The most distinctive quality of love is its desire to give. Love that seeks to get is not love. If when a woman gives herself she tries to secure individual property it will be only that she may give it to the man she loves. Marriage is a partnership of soul and body, and this includes property. It still remains true, however, that each must have in order that he may give. Besides this, there are always outside obligations, and special needs within the group, that require individual property for their realisation.

In the past, the partnership of marriage has been incomplete on the property side; why not complete it? Why not reorganise our laws and our public opinion so that two people who establish a family, putting into it all they have, should pay out of the income the necessary family expenses and divide all else equally between the parties? Property acquired before marriage, and all inherited property, might well be held in individual right since it should never be a prise for prostitution, not even when it is euphemistically termed "a good home."

Under equal suffrage Idaho has passed such a law, and all property gained after marriage belongs equally to husband and wife. If the wife dies, her heirs, in absence of a will, inherit half of the family property. If the two separate, the court, in absence of an outside agreement, settles the property as it does the children. The judge may order that it be divided equally, or he may give it all to either party, according to conditions; but the woman has identical rights with the man. Surely some such solution is demanded by our present unrest. No one will ever be economically independent; but husband and wife should be economically equal.

Women in Industry

N ALL THE animal world one can hardly find a place where orderly effort, planned to secure some future advantage, does not appear. Getting food, defending life, and caring for offspring have all combined to drive not only the descendants of Adam, but his ancestors as well, to sweat-producing effort. Of course this is not definitely planned; getting food often waits on appetite; defence is sometimes merely running away; and the young are frequently left to feed themselves or die. But the fact remains that in digging burrows, building nests, laying up honey and nuts, and in protecting and providing for the young, a vast deal of effort is put forth in forest and field which is not immediately productive of pleasure.

This work is seldom equally shared by all the members of the group With bees, the drones and the queen are alike exempt from work, and an asexual group has been developed to feed and protect them. Some ants compel others to do their work; and everywhere there seem to be individuals who are constitutionally lazy and others who, because of strength or sex attractiveness, are able to get more than their share of food and protection with less than their share of effort.

From the first, some division of work between male and female grows almost inevitably out of their different relations to reproduction. Following conception, the male can always run away and leave the female to feed and fight for herself and her offspring, and he is very prone to do so. Even when he stays by and shares in the joy of the newly born he generally leaves the female to get ready the nest, and largely she protects and provisions it.

Among domesticated animals, where their working possibilities have been very highly developed, females are much more desirable workers than males. The maternal function partly explains this, as in the case of cows and hens which give us milk and eggs; and even with mares and sheep the offspring adds to the general working value. Still, it seems to be true that even for purposes of draught, the males are of less value than the females, unless reduced to the non-sexual condition of geldings and oxen. The stallion, bull or ram is too katabolic, too much of a consuming, distributing, destroying force to be very valuable in the daily routine of agriculture or commerce. While the female is generally smaller and less powerful than the male, she is quiet, easily enslaved; and, as we have said, her maternal functions can be diverted to our daily use. She produces more workers, and her flesh is more palatable, because less distinctive, than that of the male. Hence, among domesticated animals, selection, based on considerations of work, multiplies females and keeps males only for breeding purposes.

As a quadruped, the female suffers very little handicap from the functions peculiar to her sex, except when actually carrying her young or nursing them. When she stands erect, however, the support for the special organs of reproduction is far from ideal; heavy lifting, or long-continued standing, often leads to disaster, and the periodic functions, even in the healthiest conditions, must always place women at a working disadvantage as compared with men. Add to this the fact that women are smaller, less agile, and far less strong, than men, and, even when not encumbered with young, it is clear that a woman, when confronting physical work in competition with men, needs something more than a fair field and free competition.**33** Idealists and travellers among primitive people love to tell us how easily women meet their special functions, carrying burdens equal to those carried by men when on the march, and dropping out from the caravan for only a few hours to give birth to a child; but the fact remains that women in all primitive societies age quickly and that those who are spoiled are thrown aside and forgotten.**34** Woman's handicap as a working animal in competition with man is too obvious and too deep-seated to be idealised away.

In all savage societies labour is clearly specialised between the sexes. The man, because of his superior strength and mobility, fights, hunts and makes weapons of the chase. The woman fetches and carries, digs and delves, cures the meat, makes the rude huts, clothing and pottery. Gradually she changes wild grasses to domesticated plants, and rears the young animals brought home from the chase, till they follow and serve their human masters. She is truly the mother of industries, and it in no way detracts from her credit that her motherhood is here, as elsewhere, mainly unthinking.

With the exhaustion of the supply of wild animals, man is forced to turn his attention to the world of vegetation and he takes over the direction of the plants and animals which woman has largely domesticated. In his career as fighter and hunter he has learned to cooperate with his fellows to a degree which aids him greatly in dividing the arable land, protecting his crops, and using grazing lands in common with the tribe. He has also learned to make stone hatchets, spears and bows and arrows. Woman has not felt the same necessity to invent in her work; such new tools as she has devised have been helpful, but men who could not invent have been wiped out by those who learned to make stronger spears or better arrow-heads.

It is the same difference in adaptability which one observes today between the farmers on the western frontier of America and those who remain in their peasant homes in Europe. The peasant has even greater need of inventing than has his expatriated countryman in Colorado, but he lacks the driving impulse. It was the same with women and men under the conditions of savage life. Thus it came about that man's greater strength and mobility, backed by power of cooperation and invention, gave him the leadership in such primitive life as we find depicted in the pages of Homer or in the epic of the Jews. True, woman was his first lieutenant, but he spoke for her in most of the larger matters of the industrial life.

With settled conditions and accumulation of wealth, the most desirable women were almost entirely freed from physical labour and gradually became luxury-loving parasites and playthings, as we pointed out in the second chapter of this volume. Meantime slaves were multiplying, male and female and, while the most desirable women passed to the harem, the mass of them became drudges in house and field. It is hard for us to realise that it is exactly in those times when a few women are surrounded with great luxury that most of the sex are reduced to heavy labour and wretchedness.

During the early Christian ages, a tradition was gradually formed concerning woman's place in industry, or rather three traditions were formed. The working woman of the lower classes was to be the housekeeper, which meant that she was to care for food, cook, spin, weave, sew and mend, scrub and wash, bear children and nurse and tend them. If she were of the middle class, she was to be a mother, to supervise this range of work, look after dependents, conserve social conditions and be the lady bountiful of her district. The second ideal was the woman of religion, who was to subdue her passions, observe set prayers and other religious exercises, and do the menial work of the convent. The third ideal was the lady of chivalry, who appeared after the tenth century. She was to be cared for and protected from work or anxiety; menials were to prepare her food, clothes and ornaments; gallants were to await her orders and do her bidding.

With the rise of Protestantism, and later with the rise of modern democracy, these ideals were blended, and women found themselves, not indeed slaves and subject to sale, but serfs, entangled in a mass of feudal obligations and bound to the house. Practically, most men still hold this threefold conception of woman's place in the social organism. She is to be a combination of housekeeper, nun and lady. It is the kitchen, church and children ideal of the German Emperor.

Meantime forces were set at work which were to change the economic foundations of the family and enable the woman to emerge from serfdom into some new form of industrial relationship

From the rise of the European cities in the twelfth century, certain industries have tended, especially in the Netherlands and in England, to segregate themselves in farm-houses and towns. Women naturally participated in these activities, generally taking the least desirable parts. With the freeing of the mind, which followed the democratic revolutions at the end of the eighteenth century, inventions blossomed out and perfected steam engines, cotton gins, spinning jennies, and a thousand other machines driven by steam or water power, which have changed the civilisation of Europe and America. Miss Edith Abbott has shown us how this change, involving increasing segregation and specialisation, came into America even in the pre-Revolutionary time.**35**

Spinning and weaving industries led the way in this movement, but its full force was not felt until the late eighteenth century. Since then, one industry after another has left the home for the factory until today, in all large communities, even the preparation of food increasingly goes to the packing-house, the canning establishment, the bakery and the delicatessen-store. These industries needed hands, and so the women followed them to the factories.

As 1870 marks the beginning of higher education for women, so it also marks the beginning of her industrial self-consciousness. The perfecting of such inventions as the typewriter, the telegraph and the telephone, and the creation of a great variety of office appliances, together with the perfecting of highly elaborate means of distribution, like the departmental store, called for thousands of cheap workers possessed of some slight intelligence but not necessarily having any serious preliminary training. Our elementary schools and high schools have increasingly turned out a multitude of girls who could meet these requirements. The increased cost of living, the lessened labour demands of the home, and the attractions of the pay envelope, have called millions to work in industrial plants. In 1890, there were 4,005,532 wage-earning women in the United States; in 1900, 5,319,397; while in 1910, we have probably nearly 8,000,000.

Like most other great changes in civilisation, this industrial transformation was neither preceded nor accompanied by any general consciousness of what was happening. Daily necessities were offset by weekly pay envelopes, or the failures fell out of sight, and so the next week and the years followed. Country populations moved away; cities grew enormously, leading to congestion in living which, combined with the daily absence of women, has often transformed the old time homes into communal tiers of tenements occupied, during working hours, only by the young and the infirm.

The children of all ages after a while followed their mothers into the factories; but the evil effects of child labour were so apparent that repressive legislative measures have increasingly raised the age of their admission until now, in the more advanced communities, they must stay outside the factory doors until they are twelve or fourteen years old. Some growing self-consciousness, largely of a police nature, has led us to institute measures for the protection of the children who are not allowed to work. Schools, playgrounds, day nurseries, institutional churches, college settlements and public social centres now bid against the streets and vacant lots, the nickel shows and the dancing halls, for the children's patronage.

Education, however, true to its origin as the assistant of theology, refuses to recognise in any large way the new world into which we have come, and where the next generation of children must follow. Manual training has, here and there, quieted the fears of some who had disturbing visions; and we go on employing an army of unenfranchised, celibate women, with little or no industrial experience, to teach ten million boys how to be good citizens of a republic, and how to serve in a modern industrial army; and ten million girls how to work in shops and factories, and how to live without homes. As a consequence, girls come up to the factories from their schools with ideals,**36** so far as the school has shaped them, founded on unmarried school mistresses and George Washington; and they pass, by way of the altar, into cheerless tenements which the school still thinks of as places where children are cared for, family clothing is made and the family baking is done. Practically, of course, most education is given outside the schools, and there the evils of an unregulated time of transition are multiplied through imitation.

The wealth and material comfort produced for the fortunate classes by these segregated industries have blinded us to their effects on human life, and we have all been bribed to silence concerning everything which could discourage enterprise or frighten capital. Like most bribes, however, these have largely stopped in the pockets of the exploiters of public opinion.

In the opening years of this new century, public consciousness has had a wonderful awakening.**37** The popular mind, quickened by universal education, and freed from a burden of fixed beliefs, is turning restlessly to inquire about everything that affects human life. Work could not escape this inquisition, and so we are asking not only for a fairer division of the profits of work, but we are also inquiring what occupations are unfit for women, with their special limitations and obligations. When the work is reasonable, how long should a woman work daily? Should she work at night and overtime? Should she work with dangerous machinery? Should she handle substances that endanger health? Should she be required to stand through hours of continuous work? Should she work in bad air, due to dust, moisture, or excessive heat or cold? Should she have a decent retiring-room? Some daring inquirers are even asking whether industrial efficiency, gained through specialisation and keying up, may not be purchased at too high a price of mental monotony and nervous strain. Most people are content to learn that the effects are not immediately destructive to the girls and women involved; but some day we shall demand that the barons of industry shall not be allowed to squander the heritage of the unborn generations.

Women have themselves done much to quicken this public consciousness. Enrolled in labour unions, they have shown power to stand together and make sacrifice, as in the shirt-waist makers' strike in New York in 1908, which commanded the admiration of all fair-minded observers. The more fortunately placed women have aided these movements toward self-betterment; and, through such organisations as the National Consumers' League, they have compelled manufacturers and shopkeepers to observe more reasonable hours, pay better wages, and furnish decent material conditions for their employees.**38**

The solution of woman's present industrial problem is not an easy task, but out of the present unsettlement certain facts are emerging with a good deal of clearness. The efficiency in production, secured by concentration and specialisation, make it certain that the old-time home with its multiplied industries will not return, but that more and more even of its present lessened activities will be transferred to factories and to their equivalents. It is also certain that women are not going to be supported in indolence by men, because when deprived of the discipline which full participation in life gives, they must always degenerate. For themselves, and for the sake of their children, they will demand a chance to live abundantly. It is also clear that our present chaotic conditions are destructive of health, happy marriages, effective homes, and the strong line of descendants which must always be the chief care of an intelligent society.

In the first place, then, we must work to produce an entire change in our present mental attitude toward organised industries. Our present worship of industrial products, no matter how obtained, must give way to a recognition of the fact that the chief asset of a nation is its people; that a woman is more important than the clothes she makes in factories or sells in stores; and that to needlessly destroy or scrapheap a working woman is worse than to needlessly destroy or scrapheap the finest and most costly machine ever devised by man. Such a statement seems to carry conviction in its every phrase, but the fact is that we do not believe it, and until we do believe it, there will be little help for our present absurd and wretched conditions. Unregulated competition, backed by greed of individuals and groups, will go on wasting the wealth of women's lives until we cease to be fascinated and hypnotised by the display of products which they make possible. Better fine women and children, and few things, than stores and warehouses crowded with goods, and the women and children of our present factory towns. By fixing our attention on people instead of things, we should almost certainly secure more and better things; but, regardless of cost, we must change the focus of our attention.

In the second place, girls must get ready to be women. The education of the home and the school must be unified, and together they must give a training that will lead girls into the actualities of the life that lies before them. Our present elementary schools, and still more our high schools, lead girls neither to intelligent work nor to intelligent living as women and mothers. Up to at least the age of fourteen, the education should be general, looking to the development of all the powers of body, mind and sensibilities. But through all these eight or ten years of training, two factors should receive constant and intelligent attention. In the first place, we should realise that we are not fitting women for drawing-rooms nor for convents, but for a working world; therefore well graded and interesting manual training should run through all these years and should furnish a well-developed base for later special industrial preparation of some kind. In the second place, the girls should be taught by men and women, married and unmarried, and fine ideals of actual womanhood, not alone in shops and factories, in school-rooms, and in professions — but also in homes, should be constantly held before them. Our present education leaves this training mainly to the homes, and neither the parasitic rich nor our eight million wage-earning women, when mothers, can or will attend to it.

After the girl reaches the age of fourteen, she should have at least two years of further education in which she could master the details of some necessary work which would enable her to look the world in the face and offer fair payment for her living. With most girls, this work would be connected with children and the service of the home; for domestic service, no matter how organised, must always occupy a multitude of women. All girls should have at least rudimentary training in these matters.

During the period of transition from schools to their own

family life, the girls might well give a half dozen years to work in factories and stores where the conditions should be as good, and as well guarded, as in our best school buildings — in factories, in a word, where the employers would be willing that their own daughters should work. This is surely a fair standard. Work which is not safe or fit for me to do, is not fit for me to hire done. If this principle fails, then democracy is but a dream.

But during all this period of preparation we should never forget that, as Madame Gnauck-Kühne so admirably points out, "women's work has to a large extent an episodic character."**39** All women confront romantic love, marriage and children; and any woman who misses them misses the crowning joy and glory of her life. Vicarious realisation may save the soul, but it can never fill the place of reality. The man fronts these same experiences, but they are not related to his work as they are related to the work of women. Surely there can be no doubt that the ideal solution, in this period, is a man and woman so deeply bound together by love that there is no question of self-protection, either in terms of work or money; and the man being freed from the burdens of maternity, should mainly earn the income. We shall discuss the new type of home and family in a later chapter, but in any home where there are children there is need of an intelligent mother's very constant care.

If a happy home were the universal destiny of women, our problem would be greatly simplified; but this is far from being the case. Not more than one-half of all women over fifteen are married at any one moment. From the ages of twenty to thirty-five, one-half are married; but it is only from thirty-five to fifty-five that as many as three-fourths are married; over fifty-five there are less than one-half married, and most of the others are widows.**40** Most of these women who are not married must work outside the home, and no girl, rich or poor, should be allowed to reach maturity without being prepared to face this possibility. Work is not a curse but a blessing; it is an indispensable part of every well-ordered life; and without it, the individual and the group will certainly degenerate. Rich and foolish parents, who cannot realise this basal fact, should nevertheless see that, even as insurance, their daughters must be able to pay their way in life, if need comes, without selling themselves either in marriage or out. Even if the woman marries happily, she is never sure that she may not some day have to face self-support, and possibly for more mouths than her own.

But the woman who marries during her adolescent period, between the ages of twenty-five and fifty, must also work, and here we meet the hardest problem of all. More money is often needed than the man can earn; the wife may bring an industrial or professional equipment which is too valuable to discard; often the demands of the home, especially where there are no children, do not call forth the best energies of the woman, and she needs the larger life of outside work. Hence many married women must continue to work away from the home. In any of these cases, the problem is difficult. Bearing and rearing a child should retire a mother from fixed outside occupation for at least a year. Arguments born out of conflict cannot change this primitive fact.**41** Women should not do shop or factory work during the last months of pregnancy, and babies should be nursed from seven to nine months. A baby should be nursed for twenty minutes, every two or three hours of its waking time; and since it does not always waken regularly, the nursing mother is debarred from most continuous work, even if it does not interfere with her effectiveness as a milk producer.

The question of maternal care for children after they are weaned is more difficult to settle, but notwithstanding certain statistics gathered in Birmingham,**42** in February, 1910, which showed that the infant mortality among working mothers was one hundred and ninety per thousand, while, among those not industrially employed, it was two hundred and seventy per thousand, it seems sure that infant mortality is extremely high in foundling asylums and in factory homes. In Fall River, where out of every one hundred women, forty-five are at work outside the home, three hundred and five babies, out of every one thousand born, die before they are a year old; while even in New York City, but one hundred and eighty-nine out of a thousand die. The natural location of Fall River should make it a very healthy city. One remembers, too, the classic statement that deaths among little children fell off steadily in Paris during the siege of 1870. Little children seem better off even in time of war, with the mothers at home, than in time of peace with their mothers in the factory.

A few years ago, we turned to sanitary day nurseries, and to pasteurised milk and other prepared baby foods, as the solution for neglected or unhygienic feeding. Today we know that even a dirty and ill-conditioned mother secretes better milk for her baby than can be prepared in any laboratory. We must wash the mother and feed her the milk, and then let her give it to her baby, instinct with her own life. It is quite possible that our recent talk of ignorant mother love and of the necessary substitution of sanitary nurseries, canned care and pre-digested affection must all go the same way. We shall probably get our best results by cleaning up the home, enlightening the mother, and then letting her love her child into the full possession of its human qualities.

Economically, too, at least with factory workers, it is questionable if their wages will support sanitary day-nurseries, with intelligent nurses for small groups of children, and at the same time pay some one to cook and scrub at home. If the mother must still cook and care for her house, in addition to her factory work, the burden is too great; and if money for nurses must come from the state, or from charity, then we all know the danger of such subsidies to industry, in its effect on wages.

Surely the ideal toward which we must work is for the mother, during the period when she is bearing and rearing children, to be supported by the father of her children. Let her do the work meantime which will best care for her children, and at the same time conserve and strengthen her powers for the third period of her life.

This period, from fifty to seventy-five years, is now more shamefully wasted than any other of our national resources. If one attends a State federation of women's clubs one will find nearly every delegate of this age. They are women of mature understanding and of ripe judgement, still possessing abundant health and strength, and where relieved by economic conditions from the necessity of manual work, they have to live such irregular and uncertain relations to life as can be maintained by mothers-in-law, grandmothers, club secretaries, and presidents of town improvement societies. Remove all restrictions on woman's activity, and these strong matrons would vitalise our schools, give us decent municipal housekeeping, supervise the conditions under which girls and women work in shops and factories, and do much to clean up our politics. Debarred from direct power as they are, they are still making us decent in spite of ourselves.

For the future, then, it seems that we must accept working women in every path of life. We must remove all disabilities under which they labour, and at the same time protect them by special legislation as future wives and mothers. All girls must master some line of self-supporting work; and, except in the cases of those who have very special tastes and gifts, they should select work which can be interrupted, without too great loss, by some years of motherhood. During this time, the mother must be supported so that she can largely care for her own child, though she must also maintain outside interests through work, which will keep her in touch with the moving current of her time. Industries must be humanised and made fit for women. The last third of a woman's life must be freed from legal limitations and popular prejudices, so that we may secure these best years of her life for private and public service. And meantime, it is well to remember that every step we take in making this a fit world for woman to work in, makes it a fit world for her father, her brothers, her lover and her husband to work beside her.

The Meaning of Political Life

T IS A well-known fact that when words have been long and vigorously used they gather within and around themselves varied meanings. Some parts of these meanings are remnants of historic, and possibly outworn, experience; other parts are the result of more or less deliberate perversion under the stress of deep feelings aroused by opposition and fighting. This is especially the fate of words in any way associated with politics. Think how battered and useless for purposes of ordinary discussion "democrat" and "republican" or "socialist" have become in America!

In the struggle of the last fifty years over woman's suffrage, most of the words involved have undergone such transformations; and so many prejudices have become associated with them, that no one can think or speak clearly and fairly today in these terms. "Woman's Rights," "enfranchisement," "Votes for Women," "suffragette," "polls," "ballot," "political issues," and many other words, have gone through this destructive process.

To read some of the most popular literature on this subject one might imagine that women had all deserted home and fireside, babies and baking, and were lined up, struggling fiercely to deposit certain printed slips, called votes or ballots, dealing with esoteric mysteries understood only by men like Mr. Bryan or Mr. Roosevelt, in ballot-boxes. These receptacles are supposed to be behind, or very near, lawless saloons, where gangs of hoodlums are waiting to assault the bearers of these mysterious tickets. Thus Miss Seawell writes in the *Atlantic Monthly* for September 1910: "The trouble would begin with the mere attempt of women to deposit their ballots. A dozen ruffians at a single polling-place would prevent a single woman from depositing a single vote. There can be no doubt that this means would be used by the rougher element and that the polls would become a scene of preordained riot and disorder." Of course, such statements could not appear in a leading magazine, in a land where women have been voting quietly for many years, were it not for the perversity of the words which the author tries to use, but which really use her. In other periodicals, equally respectable, one learns that women, goaded on by the intolerable political tyranny of men, have agreed as one soul to advance, with ballots in their hands, and sweep graft and greed, drink and all other human wrongs, into the sea of oblivion forever. Of course, this is nonsense, or worse, and in this chapter I should like to turn away from this warfare, leaving even the battered and prejudiced-soaked words alone, as much as may be possible, and simply ask: What is political life, not as defined in books, but as actually lived by a self-respecting farmer or merchant of our acquaintance? What qualities does political life presuppose in a participant? How does its use affect him? What does it enable him to accomplish? What is the relation of a woman — not some militant or unsexed ogre, nor a female breeding animal in a harem, but our own sisters, wives and daughters as they really are — what is their relation to this mysterious process?

If one approaches the political life of our modern democracies in this simple spirit of inquiry it would seem that the first requisite for participation is the ability to form sound judgements concerning political matters; and all matters are now becoming political which affect the welfare of the community. Certainly the citizen cannot devise political machinery nor select candidates to work such machinery, much less "cast a ballot," until he knows what he wants done. What are some of the questions, then, on which he must form judgements?

First of all, he must be prepared to think intelligently about protecting his life and property. He must know something of the danger of foreign invasion, of the consequent need of a navy and standing army. He must make up his mind whether it is necessary to spend $123,000,000 yearly on an American navy and $156,000,000 on an American army, as we are at present doing, that we may be ready to fight England, Germany or Japan if at any time we want to do so. He must ask himself whether this money might not better be used in fighting ignorance, crime, poverty and disease.

The would-be citizen must also think about protecting himself from assault as he walks about the streets; about protecting his house from thieves as he lies asleep at night. He must have thought about the careless use of cars, automobiles, firearms and explosives in general. He must consider the danger from fires, contagion, diseases, mobs; he must think intelligently about contaminated water and impure foods. All these things are necessary for the physical well-being of the community life. Of course, if either man or woman cannot think intelligently about these things, he ought not to have control of them; he should leave such matters to those who can think of them.

In the second place, the would-be citizen must have fairly sound judgements on questions of raising and spending necessary revenue. What are the effects of direct and indirect taxation? Would a heavy tax on land force unused lands, including mines and waterways, into use? Should a man with a cash income of $50,000 a year pay more to support government than one with a cash income of $500? What are the objections to an income tax? How does it work in England, where it has been fairly tried? Should a great corporation pay taxes in proportion to its wealth, and in places where the wealth is protected by the law? If so, how can it be reached? Should churches, museums, libraries and schools be taxed; if not, why not? Should taxes be laid on flour, meat and eggs, on woollen cloth, on silks, velvets, ostrich plumes and diamonds? Should taxes be laid on whiskey, wines, tobacco, cigars and race-tracks? Should taxes be devised, or continued, to protect such infant industries as now handle our kerosene oil, meat, sugar and steel? Surely no one who cannot form independent judgements on these matters should presume to direct them through voting.

But not only must a nation raise revenue in the wisest and most equitable manner possible, and spend it effectively and economically, but it must also care for its present possessions. So the would-be citizen must know about the wealth in which he wants to share. What do the national, State and municipal governments own? How should the vast domains of land, the onetime inexhaustible forests, the mines of coal and metal, the waterways and water-powers, the special privileges and franchises belonging to the people be used? Should they be thrown away, gambled away, given away as favours, rented, sold, or handled directly by the people? On what terms or under what guarantees should they be turned over to individuals or companies, if this is to be done? Those who cannot form judgements on these matters should not be entrusted with such vast responsibility, be they men or women.

Questions of our foreign relations must also occupy the thought of the citizen. Are foreign entanglements necessary or desirable? If so, with what European or Asiatic nations should we seek to strengthen our friendship? Are our interests nearly identical with those of England? If we formed a close defensive alliance with her should we be thereby aiding universal peace as much as we might by maintaining more generally friendly relations with all European powers? Would an alliance with England probably draw us into her troubles, if she has any, in Egypt or India? How would such an alliance affect our relation with England's present ally, Japan? Are we fitted by the genius of our institutions and by our experience to handle a foreign empire? If not, what should we do with the Philippines?

So, too, those who are to direct the destinies of the country must think out what our relations are to be with Latin America. In the past some statesman, a Richelieu or a Bismarck, had a policy and led his nation to it by devious paths of indirection. But now that each citizen is a king, he must have a policy for his realm. Are our republican neighbours to the south to be increasingly recognised as under our protection and direction? If so, how are we to maintain the peace and secure payment of their foreign debts? All these problems are bound up with the management of the Panama Canal. They confront us in different forms in connection with immigration, especially of Asiatics.

Our institutional life must also be regulated by the citizens, and so they must have judgements about each of its details. They must know what they think about the family, forms of legal marriage and divorce, and the care of children when the family fails. The Church must be considered and protected; possibly it should be encouraged; and possibly its unwarranted assumption should sometimes be checked. Schools must be founded, supported, directed. Art galleries, museums and clubs must be chartered, and then controlled; and so must all the other institutions of our modern society. The would-be citizen must be able to think about all this work.

Industries, on which our individual and collective well-being depend, must be encouraged by special favours, limited to the public good, protected from violence, inspected in the interest of employees. Hours must be regulated, disputes settled, conditions of labour and safety secured. Children should be protected against employers' greed; and working women must receive special consideration, if the race of strong men is to continue. Here again the citizen must have judgements, or the power to make judgements, as new needs arise.

Then, too, there is a tradition of government, established by the fathers and modified by experience, which should be understood by the citizens. It recognises certain rights as being reserved by the individual States, and others as belonging to the national government. The would-be citizen should be acquainted with this tradition so that he can determine how far it is desirable to adopt a new nationalism. He will have to pass judgement on the control of interstate commerce, national or State control of public lands, national divorce and liquor laws, national food inspection, and other practical subjects which may destroy the older balance of power so jealously guarded by our earlier statesmen. The citizen must make up his mind if this is desirable.

Newer political theories must also receive the citizens' attention. Many people believe that wealth created by the people can be enjoyed by the people only when they control the sources of supply and the means of production and distribution. The citizen should know whether these socialist tendencies should be favoured or suppressed. There are others who believe that government is unnecessary, and that men and women can be happy and effective only when formal laws are abrogated. The citizen must determine whether he will allow those who hold such doctrines to express them; or whether he will suppress their meetings and forbid them to enter the country. These are but a few of the subjects concerning which the citizen must think, but they are typical and they may represent the rest.

In the last analysis, it is these judgements on political matters which govern a modern democracy, whatever the laws on the statute books may be, and whatever machinery of government may be established.

Not long since, I visited one of our States where the laws forbid any one to make or sell, as a beverage, any intoxicating liquors, within the State. At the leading hotel, in the large city where I stopped, beer and whiskey signs were displayed outside the entrance; and at an open bar, in the centre of the hotel, four bartenders were dispensing all kinds of drinks, while at the tables of the hotel restaurant, liquors were openly bought and drunk. There are many indictments standing against this hotel, but in two test cases juries have refused to convict the proprietors. I am told it is the same in all of the principal hotels in the larger cities of this State. In this same State, the laws forbid the manufacture or sale of cigarettes, but they are openly displayed and sold in nearly all cigar stores. In the same State, whites and blacks live under the same laws, but blacks seldom vote; they do not use the parks, attend white people's meetings nor ride with the whites in public conveyances. And yet the city was quiet and orderly and I felt as safe in person and property as though the laws on the statute books, instead of the judgements in the public mind, were being obeyed. Since this form of public opinion is so powerful, it is well that it should be intelligent.

Granted, then, that the candidate for citizen honours is prepared to pass judgement on such matters as we have indicated, he must next be prepared to devise and control means to carry these judgements into effect. Here he approaches the problems of statecraft. He must have in his mind a general scheme of government, with a sense of legislative, judicial and executive functions. He must realise the value of a constitution, as a point of departure; and have a theory as to safe ways of modifying it. He must have fairly clear notions of legislation, and of the kinds of laws that are desirable and effective. He should know how far representative legislative bodies can be trusted to express the will of the people; and he should have studied the working of the initiative and the referendum. It is also desirable that he should know the theory of two chambers, and should have ideas as to how the members of the second chamber, if there is to be one, should be chosen.

The candidate for citizen honours should know something of the organisation of the judicial branch of government. He should know something of the powers and duties of local magistrates, of county, State and national courts. He should recognise the difference between civil and criminal jurisdiction. He should have an opinion as to whether judges should be elected or appointed, and if appointed, who should select them. He should realise the grave dangers that surround a corrupt judiciary, and he should know the means by which a court is enabled to maintain its standing and authority.

So of the executive power, he should see its relation to the other powers, from the constable to the president. He should know the qualities required in a good executive and should be able to distinguish them in possible candidates. He should know that when the executive is lax the best of laws fall into abeyance, and he should know how such officers can be held up, through criticism by public opinion and penalties, to the fulfilment of duties. The recall should have been considered.

In the third place, the citizen should know how to select the right kind of people to carry his political judgements into effect. Possibly, under a representative form of government, this is the most necessary qualification for a good voter. Many of the matters with which modern government must deal are technical, and the citizen here, as in his private affairs, must rest on the judgement of those he employs. And yet, in general, he must know what he wants.

He must know the general laws that govern the organisation of parties; and he should be somewhat acquainted with the psychology of crowds. He should know how candidates are selected under the convention or caucus system; he should have an independent judgement on direct primaries.

In selecting men, the citizen must be able to recognise general ability and intellectual fitness. It is at this point that modern democracies are most apt to go wrong. The standards by which we measure men and women are most imperfect; and we are prone to let one good or bad quality overshadow all others. Thus in an extended study on school children's attitude toward Queen Victoria in England, and toward President McKinley in America, made while these rulers were alive, we found that less than twenty per cent mentioned any kind of political ability, nor did they often mention their general ability, nor their honesty. They admired them primarily because they were "good and kind." In other words the school children of these two lands approve their rulers because, in a vague general way, they like them.**43** The significance of the study lies in the fact that in all democracies a large number of the voters live on an intellectual plane represented by these school children.

This conclusion is borne out by the judgement of Miss Jane Addams who, writing of foreign voters about Hull House, says: "The desire of the Italian and Polish and Hungarian voters in an American city to be represented by 'a good man' is not a whit less strenuous than that of the best native stock. Only their idea of the good man is somewhat different. He must be good according to their highest standard of goodness. He must be kind to the poor, not only in a general way, but with particular and unfailing attention to their every want and misfortune. Their joys he must brighten and their sorrows he must alleviate. In emergency, in catastrophe, in misunderstanding with employers and with the law, he must be their strong tower of help Let him in all these things fill up their ideal of the 'good man' and he has their votes at his absolute disposal."**44**

To be a safe citizen one must be able to go beyond this kindly feeling and ask, Does the candidate know enough to do what I want done? Has he the honesty to resist the temptation to exploit me? Has he the leadership to command the best efforts of the subordinates in his department? Has he serious defects that may cause his failure? Is he an opportune man for the time and place?

This selection is made very difficult today by the misrepresentation of interested individuals and political parties; and especially by the reports in the press, which seek to discredit candidates they oppose, and to gloss over or deny defects in their chosen leaders. Thus the whole public atmosphere in the midst of a campaign is intended to confuse and bewilder the citizen who is honestly seeking the best candidate. Only ripened intelligence, experience with men and women, and ability to judge conflicting evidence, can enable the voter to select wisely.

In the last place, if the citizen knows what he wants, how to devise the governmental machinery to get it, and how to select the right men to see that it is done, he must register his desire by a vote; and then watch his servant carefully to see if he justifies the trust imposed in him. If he does not, then the citizen must criticise, threaten, and, if necessary, finally dismiss the unfaithful employee. Only one who can fulfil all these functions can be considered a desirable citizen from the point of view of a modern democracy. "Eternal vigilance is the price of liberty."

And why should one desire to undertake this arduous responsibility? In the first place, because he wants the public work well done, as he understands it; and the only way to have it done in this manner is to attend to it himself. If he does not attend to it, some one else will do so; and if the intelligent citizens do not look after it then the public business will be exploited by individuals, or groups, in their own interest; and, before the citizen realises what is happening, he will be deprived of that political liberty to secure which millions of men and women have struggled and suffered and even given their lives in the years which lie behind us.

And yet possibly the most important value of participation in political life today is the byproduct of continuous education which it gives. Modern political life has probably done more to train the men involved in it than have schools or churches. Business and industries alone might claim to be its rivals. In a despotism, all the events of public life are uncertain and seemingly accidental, depending as they do on the caprice of an individual. This discourages thought among the masses, paralyzes action, and breeds inertia and hopelessness. At best, it gives rise to periods of desperation and violence; at its worst, it gives us the hopeless masses of Mohammedan lands. In a free democracy, on the other hand, those who participate are in a continuous process of education, judging, selecting, willing, and always with regard to realities that affect daily life. Citizenship gives one a continuous laboratory course of training in the art of right living.

Nor can the full value of this continuous training be obtained by the onlooker, no matter how intelligent he may be. For full growth of mind and spirit one must participate; just as in athletics one must leave the spectator's bench and play the game if one would develop one's own powers. Participation means love, hate, devotion and sacrifice, and only when all these powers of the soul are brought into play, together with the judgement, is the character strengthened and life more abundantly obtained.

It must be evident to any one who has carefully followed this analysis that hardly any of the adult male voters in our modern democracies have the qualifications of good citizens. How, then, is good government achieved? It is not achieved. We have very bad government. Everywhere there is waste and inefficiency. Wealth is unjustly divided; great corporations seize public utilities and exploit them for private gain; enormous sums are squandered on unnecessary and dangerous battleships and soldiers; in building a single State Capitol, $3,500,000 was recently stolen, not only wasting public wealth, but corrupting public morals; in some parts of our land little children still drive the wheels of industry; and it is everywhere cheaper to scrap-heap men and women than machines; most of our cities are ugly and badly ruled; drunkenness, gambling and prostitution are common; life is not always secure from lawless attack; and the machinery of justice is clogged and moves slowly. Part of our intelligent adult population has no direct share in the government under which it must live. We have just such a government as we should expect where incompetent people decide such vast issues of life.

But, on the other hand, we are vastly better off than any great people has ever been before us. The mistakes are our own; they are made by us who participate in government, and we are learning from them. Those who exploit us may be called to account; and frequently they are caught and punished. Of those who stole the millions in Harrisburg, nearly a score have died disgraced, or are in prison or exile; and $1,300,000 has been returned to the treasury of the State. Even when those who betray us are not caught red-handed we learn to distrust and then to despise them. They pass their last years in exile, and when their statues are erected in our State Houses they are memorials of shame. Thus we learn the art of living, we who participate in political action.

The whole business of a modern democracy is to educate itself through doing, and we are all at school. If the bills are heavy, they are our bills; and we are steadily learning how to make them less. In the past no one learned. "The Bourbons learned nothing, and forgot nothing;" and the common people were too discouraged to think. It is on these lines that our modern democracies must be judged, not as efficient and economical political machines, but as educational institutions. Judged by this standard, we believe ourselves to be the triumph of the ages.

Nor can it be possible for people to enter political life fully prepared for its duties. Even when a young man approaches a business career we do not ask that he shall possess a knowledge of the business before beginning. If he has general preparation, and a desire to learn, he is admitted to share in its responsibilities, and then learns as he goes along. It is the same in political life; few young men at twenty-one or foreigners at the time of naturalisation, have the knowledge indicated in the preceding pages. If they have general preparation and a desire to learn, we admit them to participation, and they learn through doing.

Years ago, while discussing education with an English statesman, he asked whom I considered the leaders of education in his country. Knowing his Tory instincts, I replied, "Bradlaugh, Annie Besant, William T Stead, John Burns and Keir Hardie." He laughed contemptuously: "Why those people," he said, "are merely educating themselves in public." The statement was true and far-reaching; that is what we are all doing in our modern democracies; and that is at the same time our weakness and our glory.

Woman's Relation to Political Life

N DISCUSSING WOMAN'S right to vote it is well to remember that the right to rule, which is implicit in the right to vote, has always been limited by conditions of birth, residence, wealth, morality or intelligence. Universal manhood suffrage has never yet been achieved, and probably never will be. Under the best Greek conditions, it was only the free-born citizen, residing in his native city state, who voted. In both Greece and Rome, the suffrage was limited to classes defined by social position, wealth or military service. In our modern democracies there have always been limitations of birth, which might be overcome by naturalisation; of residence, which could be overcome by living for a certain time in a locality; of wealth, which was supposed to insure a stake in the communal well-being; and of morals and intelligence, which at least shut out criminals, the insane and the imbeciles.

Thus the right to vote is not the same thing as the right to live; and even in a commonwealth founded on ideal justice only those having a stake in the community life, and possessing normal intelligence and morality, will be allowed to rule. In a word, equal suffrage is possible, while universal man or woman suffrage is not.

All through our colonial period women had a large influence in determining community questions, and in Massachusetts, under the old Providence Charter, they voted for all elective officers for nearly a hundred years. Here and there women — like Margaret Brent, of Maryland; Abigail Adams, of Massachusetts; or Mrs. Corbin, of Virginia — put forward their right to participate in the public life around them. But, in 1776, women were not voting, and the Federal Constitution left the matter of determining electoral rights to the several States. They all decided for male suffrage.

The initial impulse to secure suffrage for American women came from Europe. After the Revolution, Frances Wright, a young Scotchwoman, came to America to lecture and write, claiming equal political rights with men. In 1836, Ernestine L Rose came from Poland and also advocated equal political rights. All the teachings of the American Revolution had favoured the idea of human equality; and, as has been pointed out, when, with established peace after the War of 1812, women engaged in anti-slavery, temperance and allied movements, they were driven by the logic of events to demand the suffrage.

In 1848, the women of the country began to organise. Mrs Elizabeth Cady Stanton, Lucretia Mott and Martha C Wright called together at Seneca Falls, New York, the first convention in America to further equal suffrage. No permanent organisation was founded, but in 1850 a convention was held in Salem, Massachusetts, and in 1852 a Woman's Rights Convention was called in Syracuse, New York, with delegates present from eight States and Canada. Miss Susan B Anthony had meantime joined the movement; and from this time on conventions and appeals became common.

The Civil War distracted attention from all social and political issues but one. The Equal Rights Association turned its attention mainly to the rights of negroes; and in 1869 the National Woman's Suffrage Association was organised to work exclusively for woman's rights. Backed by such women as Susan B Anthony, Lucy Stone and Julia Ward Howe, and aided by men like Henry Ward Beecher, the association became a national power. In 1890, the two organisations were united under the name of The National American Woman's Suffrage Association. This organisation still leads the movement in America.**45**

In 1902, an international meeting was called in Washington; and in 1904 the International Suffrage Alliance was formed in Berlin with Mrs Carrie Chapman Catt as president. Thirteen nations are now affiliated with the Alliance; and the women of the world are highly organised to further equal suffrage.

Two generations of women have given themselves to this movement, and a third still faces it. To the first group belong those leaders we have already named: Emma Willard, Elizabeth Cady Stanton, Julia Ward Howe, Susan B Anthony and their associates. It was their problem to secure woman's control of her own body and property, some share in the direction of her children, and some opportunity to train her own mind and earn an independent living. These women bore the heat and burden of a conflict in which all the blind prejudices of a fixed regime were strongly massed, presenting few promising points of attack. It is small wonder that some of these leaders gained a reputation for being hard, dogmatic, aggressive, and sometimes careless of popular sensibilities. The first generation of reformers in any field must be made of stern stuff; and their beneficiaries are apt to forget the conditions that justified means no longer necessary.

The lives of these women could not be expected to fully illustrate the type of life they hoped to see their sisters living when opportunity was finally won. Only women who participated in this struggle could fully appreciate the splendid devotion of these lives to the service of a group many of whom, being personally comfortable, were insensible to the needs of less fortunate women; and were sometimes even willing to fight back any advanced ideas which might disturb their own comfort. The feeling within this group of leaders, and the failure of oncoming generations of American women to recognise the debt of obligation they owe to its efforts, was illustrated by an incident that came up in connection with the Third International Congress of Women which met in London in 1899. The session was opened in Westminster Town Hall, with seven hundred delegates present, representing the most thoughtful women of the world. Lady Aberdeen was in the chair, and Mrs Creighton, wife of the late Bishop of London, was reading a paper. In the midst of deep attention, a door at the rear of the platform was gently opened, and Miss Susan B Anthony stepped onto the stage. She had just arrived from America. Her strong figure was bent with the weight of years; her face was squared by the conflict and partial ostracism she had met; but her glance had lost none of its stern kindliness, and her bearing none of its indomitable courage. As she appeared, this most representative audience of women in the world sprang to its feet and burst into wild cheering. In vain did Lady Aberdeen rap for order and beg the audience to let Mrs Creighton proceed. Not until Miss Anthony came to the front and urged the women to sit down was quiet restored. These women knew the price of a life which their champion had paid for their opportunities.

A few months after this the school children of the prosperous city of Rochester, NY, where Miss Anthony had been a leading citizen for many years, were asked to write school compositions in which they named the person they would most wish to be like. Over three thousand girls, in the elementary grades, wrote these papers, but not one chose Miss Anthony. This first generation of women reformers could not establish the type of womanhood for the modern world; they had not the leisure, nor the freedom, nor could they see all that lay in the future. But all the more, because their lives were hard, should they be held in grateful remembrance.

To the second generation of leaders belong women like Alice Freeman Palmer, Mary Sheldon Barnes and Charlotte Perkins Gilman. They came on the scene when the first campaign had been won; they could command their own bodies and property; college doors were swinging open where they could secure the training that should fit them for the struggle to win educational, industrial, social and political opportunity for all their sisters. They were still looked upon as blue-stockings and queer; they had often to serve as the butt of ridicule; but they had education, income, a certain degree of leisure, and a social recognition which, if grudging in some quarters, was all the more generous in others.

With the rapid development of higher education, these women found themselves associated with large groups of independent women who could create a society of their own in advanced centres of population. There was still much to be done in securing opportunity for women; but they could go on establishing the type of life that free women were to live. Their problems were, however, even more complex than those which confronted their predecessors. What line of education should women pursue? What lines of work could they best undertake? How could they combine an independent professional or industrial career with the life of a home and the responsibilities of a mother? How far must older social restraints be modified in the interest of intellectual and industrial freedom? It was a time for constructive statesmanship, rather than for revolution; and each woman knew she was under criticism, and that her success or failure was vastly more than her own personal concern. In her all free women were being judged.

To the third generation belongs the host of women who are today filling our college halls, managing the women's clubs, teaching the state schools, and competing with men in every industrial calling. Theirs is the task of completing woman's social and political emancipation, and of educating them to meet their newfound liberties. It is possible that this present generation has a keener sense of rights than of duties; and the young women of today must be led to realise that the delicate adjustments still to be worked out require devotion equal to that of the earlier generations, if the toll of wasted life is not to be excessive.

What now is the relation of women to the range of political activity described in the last chapter? Have they need of the protection which government gives? Are they able to form political judgements? Have they knowledge of the working of political machinery; or, lacking it, are they prepared to obtain it? Are they able to make a wise selection of people to represent them in political action? Have they need of the training which participation in political life gives? Have they the preliminary preparation to take up that training to advantage, and can they undertake these duties without serious loss of qualities desirable in women?

Women certainly have need of protection; each has a life dear to her, and honour which is dearer to her than life. In this respect she has a greater need than men. Most women, also, have property of some kind, and we are increasingly recognising their right to control this for themselves; hence they need property protection the same as men. We do not need to think of Mrs Sage, Mrs

Harriman, Miss Gould or Mrs Green, in this connection, for in every community we now have many women who are immediately responsible for large property interests which new legislation might affect most seriously.

In matters of institutional regulation by government, women are at least as vitally interested as men. In all that touches the family, marriage, or divorce, women have more at stake than men; and there are as many wives as husbands involved. The schools are also nearer to women than to men; more girls than boys attend them; more women are teachers; and more women than men are interested parents of school children. The church is also more vital to women today than to men. On the side of industries, it is clear that our 8,000,000 independent wage-earning women have a desperate stake in all governmental action touching the regulation of working conditions. In whatever concerns general sanitation, safe water, and pure foods, all are equally interested who must breathe and eat to live. Surely the need of women for political protection is quite as great as that of men.

In the matter of forming political judgements, not even the wisest men are beyond improvement. International affairs, monetary systems, the best way of raising taxes, and similar problems, often divide the male electorate pretty evenly into rival parties. Since both cannot be right, a great deal of poor political thinking must be done by the present body of voters. Meantime, women are showing their ability to deal intelligently with all sorts of subjects in our educational institutions, in business and in social life. Their judgements command respect in every other field; and it is hard to see why they could not apply their powers to political questions.

We must remember, too, that during these last years the field of political life has been rapidly broadening, through the awakening of social consciousness among the people. To concern one's self with politics now is to be interested in good market facilities, in rapid transit for cities, in recreation centres for children, in honest labelling of food products, in reformation of criminals, in preventing marriage among the unfit, and in a hundred similar matters. Here women will doubtless bring us a strong addition to our political efficiency. They have long been considered the natural directors of social life and, in spite of being disfranchised, they mainly handle such matters at present. Now that these subjects are being brought into the political field, women should follow them there, as they have followed their industries from the homes into the factories. There is no reason to believe that their judgements will be less sound than those of their brothers and husbands.

Of course, women's knowledge of means and methods is much less than that of men in their own class. Not only have they not participated in political life, but they have been steadily warned away from that particular tree of knowledge. Yet the present generation of women has gone through the same preliminary education in schools with its brothers; and many women in high schools and colleges have made a more extended study of political institutionalism. Still more important, more than a million women have been educating themselves for some years in this direction through voluntary associations of some kind; while in most States they have had some political practice through limited suffrage, and in a few States full experience.

In selecting representatives to carry out their will, women have certain obvious defects of temperament and training. Having been brought up for generations to judge men only as providers of sustenance and fathers of children, they must at first find it difficult to consider candidates impersonally. Still, their general morality and their standards of right are probably superior to those of men, and they are more intolerant of faults, and they find it harder to compromise on matters of character than do men. One can hardly believe that 1,700 women could be found among the respectable, church-going, American-born residents in any county of America, who would sell their votes, year after year, as that number of men voters has recently confessed to doing in Adams County, Ohio. In fact, Judge Blair says: "There was one class of the population which rebelled against the practice. It was the womanhood of Adams County, which had never become reconciled to the custom, and whose continual hostility has resulted finally, I hope, in its abolishment."**46**

Of the need of women for the training which participation in political life gives there can be no doubt. Their lives have always been directly dependent upon other individuals, and they are prone to think in small details. Any training which extends the horizon of their interests and enables them to deal more largely with these details will fit them better for living in a world where industrial, business and social changes are so rapidly merging details in larger wholes. Experience in selecting candidates for public office would also do much to broaden women's judgements of life, and would help to break down the pettiness which sometimes characterises their personal relations.

In the case of women, the community has a double reason for desiring that they shall develop political judgements and become acquainted with political methods. It is not only that they may share in the general intelligence and carry their fair part of the political burdens; but they have become the teachers, both in homes and schools, of the oncoming generation of male voters. We no longer live in small communities where children can see the simple processes of government operating around them, but in a complex civilisation where it must all be interpreted to them, and mainly by women. Many boys who complete our elementary schools never work a day under the direction of a man. In the homes, busy fathers increasingly turn over the training of children to their wives. How can these women train safe citizens for the future if they do not understand the processes involved well enough to use them themselves?

Meantime the old arguments against woman suffrage are too outworn to need serious attention. In the past decades our civilisation has become so complex, with so many groups carrying on differentiated functions, that even if we had not the millions of educated, property-owning, wage-earning, voting women that now fill our public life, the old arguments would still be obsolete. The issues of life are no longer primarily military, and but a fraction of men voters is capable of meeting modern requirements as policemen and soldiers; in time of crisis, all men would be called into the reserves; but in such periods women have always fought in the breach, from Carthage to Paris. Still, in modern warfare, those who guard the rear and furnish supplies are as necessary as those who go to the front.

It has also long been recognised that women who rear finest sons and daughters must sometimes turn away from the cradle to refresh their lives with the touch of other interests. It has also been demonstrated a thousand times over that women do not incite the lawless element to riot about the polls; but that, instead, their presence tends to remove the polling-place from the saloon and make it safer for men to go there on election-day. The plea that women would introduce a new element of sex into politics, thereby confounding its real issues, is certainly not well grounded. Sex has always played a great part in politics, as it has in all the vital affairs of life. In the open competitions of education, business or politics, sex ceases to be as significant as it is in the drawing-room.

Nor do thoughtful people imagine today that if women participated in political life they would suddenly bring about a reign of universal peace and righteousness. It has taken many centuries for men to learn to play the game of politics indifferently well as they do. The first effect of woman's participation would probably be to lower the efficiency of the electorate in some directions; but they are starting much farther along than men began, and they would learn more rapidly than men have learned.

It is often claimed that women do not want to vote; and, of course, there are many who do not care to assume such arduous and often difficult duties, if they can avoid it. The same holds true of many intelligent, but selfish men who desire the advantages of good government without its burdens. All such must be urged to do their duty to the state. Those who have vision and a large sense of duty can be trusted to do their fair part in caring for the public welfare. Those who wish to enjoy the benefits of peace and settled government, participating in the advantages of education, engaging in business, and having their persons and property protected, without sharing the burdens of government, should be forced to play their part.

If a woman should board a street-car today and, when asked for her fare, should hide her face with womanly modesty and declare that she did not wish to be involved in such public matters, but preferred that the man swinging on the strap before her should pay, she would be informed that all who use the cars must pay for their maintenance. Women in America now have more than their share of education and leisure. If they do not wish to pay their fair proportion of service, they should withdraw from the high schools and colleges, from literature and music, from offices and factories, and not crowd into places where they are unwilling to play the game. The woman who leads the movement against equal suffrage in England has made a fortune in the open market as a writer, protected by the national copyrights; she maintains a house where she is protected in person and property by the city of London, the organisation and administration of which calls for the constant attention of all intelligent citizens; and yet she urges women to take what they can get, but to refrain from doing their fair share of the city and national housekeeping, lest they lose their feminine charm. Surely those who profit by government should give their share of service.

It is idle to claim that equal suffrage will make no change in women. It will certainly accentuate the changes already made by higher education and by a freer business life. Some loss there must inevitably be in any such far-reaching change. We lost something of chivalry and of the spirit of *noblesse oblige* in the transition from feudalism to democracy. In transferring causes of personal difference from the duelling field to the courts of law, we lost a degree of poetic feeling and tragic exaltation, of personal initiative and physical courage. So when women passed from slavery to serfdom we lost something of male dominance and of female submission. We shall lose something in the present transition; but one must be content to lose Louis XIV and Versailles if one thereby finds modern France; one must be satisfied to lose an institution which gave us the tragically pathetic death of Alexander Hamilton, if it increases human justice and saves fathers to their families. We must even be content to lose the languishing and weeping lady of chivalry, and the coquetting, crocheting and confiding maiden of the eighteenth century if we gain in return fair minded comrades in daily living, devoted partners in family life, and strong, intelligent mothers for the coming generations. The sex instinct needs no fostering; it has led us to our best developments in civilisation; and its work has only begun.

So far we have taken the popular position, and have discussed this matter as though it were still in the period of debate. The fact is, it long ago passed from the field of theory; it is now a condition. In six of our States, women have now full participation in managing public affairs. In Wyoming, since 1869; in Colorado, since 1893; in Idaho, since 1896; in Washington, beginning in 1910; and in California, since 1911, women have been sharing the vote with men. In twenty-nine States they have school suffrage, and in many places municipal suffrage.**47** In newer parts of the world, like New Zealand and Australia, women have complete suffrage, while in old countries, like Norway, Sweden and Finland, they have essentially all the rights of men. In England, there are 1,141 women on Boards of Guardians and 615 on Educational Committees; and they are demanding full participation in all political life. In Canada they have school and municipal suffrage. It is no longer a time for argument; it is time for adjustment.

Meantime the results of woman's full participation in political life, even where they have had the suffrage for some years, are difficult to determine, because of the fact already pointed out that political life in a modern democracy is so closely bound up with all the other life about it. It is quite as difficult to estimate these effects as it would be to estimate the effects of housekeeping or of woman's special costume. And yet some results are clear enough to have a large bearing on the extension of woman's suffrage in new localities.

In 1906, the Collegiate Equal Suffrage League engaged Miss Helen Sumner to make a careful study of the actual working of equal suffrage in the State of Colorado. Miss Sumner, aided by several assistants, spent nearly two years in the investigation.

She gathered and carefully analysed written answers to an extended set of questions from 1,200 representative men and women of Colorado, some opposing and some favouring equal suffrage; and she and her assistants interviewed many more. They also made a general study of industrial conditions and of legislation for the State as a whole, and a detailed study of election records and newspaper files for representative cities and counties. Her report is a masterpiece of patient research and scientific exposition.**48**

Equal suffrage goes back to 1893 in Colorado; and while the influence of women has been in no way revolutionary, this report shows that, on the whole, political conditions have improved and woman's intelligence and her general public spirit have increased with no appreciable loss in distinctive feminine charm. One cannot help feeling as one reads this report that it is what a disinterested observer would have to say about the effect of woman's larger educational or industrial life since 1870.

In all democracies it is difficult to bring voters to the polls unless, as in some Swiss cantons, they are fined for absence. In Colorado, Miss Sumner shows that women cast about forty per cent. of the total vote in the earlier years of their enfranchisement, though they were in a minority of the total population.**49** In the work of the primaries they were in a much smaller minority, except when some special problem or candidate appealed to them. The more intelligent the community, the larger the woman's vote; and it is largest of all in the best residence districts of Denver, the capital city. The vote of American born women is larger than that of foreigners; and while the prostitutes of Denver have been voted in the interests of the party in power, public opinion is steadily making this more difficult. In Idaho, all residents of the red light district have been disfranchised by statute; and practically they do not vote.

There is no appreciable tendency on the part of women to form a new party, nor to favour their own sex. They are more inclined than men to scratch the ticket and, as illustrated in the case of Judge Lindsey, they sometimes rally efficiently around an independent candidate, especially on a moral issue. On the whole, women vote with their husbands, just as sons vote with their fathers; but the strength of the family vote, as compared with the vote of unsettled people, is certainly desirable.

Since the beginning of equal suffrage, Colorado has fully held her own with other States in advanced legislation, especially in social and educational lines. Women have suffered no insult at the polls, and on the whole polling-places have improved; but how far this is due to women's presence no one can say. Women have occasionally held legislative and executive offices; but they have especially distinguished themselves as State and county superintendents of schools.

When it comes to estimating the effect of voting on the women themselves, it is still harder to form an opinion. A large majority of those reporting to Miss Sumner think that women have become more intelligent and more public-spirited, but some doubt it. Morally, they have shown themselves less corrupt than men; but a considerable number think women as a whole have suffered some deterioration. This is a question bound up with our deepest feelings and our most conservative ideals; and it is inevitable that some observers should find any change for the worse. On the whole, belief in equal suffrage seems to have increased in Colorado during the twelve years under survey. Probably the results are much what they would be if one were to study a group of the most intelligent and refined men in the same community.

During the summer of 1911, I spent a month in the State of Idaho; and as I had long been interested in the problem of equal suffrage, both in England and America, I seized eagerly on the opportunity to study its practical workings at first hand. On the streets and in the tram-cars, in hotel lobbies and in lecture halls, when dining out or when making a call, few people escaped inquisition. I interviewed working men and women, men of affairs, ranchers, sheep raisers and miners, doctors, lawyers, teachers, ministers and practical politicians, both men and women.

The thing that first impresses one who has been intimately in touch with the excited and turbulent condition of mind among the English suffragettes, and the sustained and often impassioned feeling of Eastern suffrage leaders, is the absence of any burning interest in the subject on the part of men or women in Idaho. In London or New York, a suffrage inquirer would constantly strike "live wires;" in Idaho, every one is insulated. The subject is no more an issue than civil service reform or state versus national control of banking systems. Most people have even forgotten the passage of the constitutional amendment conferring equal suffrage, in 1896. Since then, men and women have gone on voting and holding office until the woman's right has become as commonplace as, and no more interesting or questionable than, the vote of any busy citizen in New Jersey.

The first question that one raises is naturally whether women do actually vote and hold office in Idaho. To answer this question, there is no body of statistics available. Every one, however, declares that they pretty generally vote. On account of long distances in the country side, they poll less votes than men, especially if the weather is bad. Probably about three-quarters as many women as men go to the polls. Often I met women who said that they did not care for the vote, and sometimes one who said she thought women ought not to vote; but these same women often added that since they had the responsibility they felt it their duty to cast a ballot; and no woman told me that she did not fulfil the obligation.

In the first legislature which met after the granting of equal suffrage, that of 1898, three women were seated, Mrs Hattie F Noble, Clara L Cambell, and Mary A Wright; Mrs Wright afterward became chief clerk of the House. In 1908, another woman, Mrs Lottie J McFadden, was returned; but there was no woman in the last legislature, and so far as I can learn, only these four have taken part in law-making. When asked why, after the first ardour of emancipation, women have taken so little part in legislation, most people said it was because they had found the work and conditions surrounding it unsuited to them. It seems generally agreed, however, that a woman could be elected to the legislature at any time if she represented a cause which needed to be brought before the people through that body.

Theorists have always insisted that equal suffrage would greatly improve the material conditions which surround the polls on election day. One of the prominent political leaders in Idaho, who has been intimately in touch with conditions for a quarter of a century, said that of course there had been great improvement in the last fifteen years. "Things would have improved any way," he said, "but I am sure that the women have had a large influence. No woman has ever been insulted at the polls in Idaho and she runs no more danger of annoyance than she would in buying her ticket at a railway window. Men are not always sober in either place; but if a man made a remark to a woman that was not polite, or used annoying language in her presence, he would be mobbed by the men even in the roughest mining camp in the State." Doubtless women have helped to break the connection between the saloon and the polling-place, but no one claims that women have made voting into a drawing-room ceremony. On the contrary, women are very persistent workers at the polls, seeking to direct doubtful voters.

Advocates of equal suffrage have pretty generally held the belief that if women were given the ballot their superior moral standards would lead to a marked change in the handling of such problems as the liquor traffic and the control of red light districts. Of woman's superior moral standards there can be no doubt; of the actual effect of her vote upon these questions there is a great deal of doubt. While I was in Idaho, the question of local option came up before the voters of Salt Lake City, in the neighbouring equal suffrage State of Utah, and the "wets" won by a vote of 14,775 to 9,162. Thousands of women must have voted for license to bring about this result. In April, 1911, the question of license or no license was voted on in Boise. In this case again the "wets" won by a considerable majority.

Take another case. For several years in Boise, until 1909, the red light district was segregated in two alleys in the heart of the city. In the municipal election of that year this issue came fairly before the voters, and the democratic nominee for mayor, who was pledged to break up the system, was elected by a considerable majority, though the city is strongly republican. This result was undoubtedly due to the women's vote. After two years, the issue came up again; and the republican nominee, who was opposed to the scattering policy though not pledged to segregation, was elected; and this result must again have been due to the woman's vote. Prominent women of the city told me that during the two years when the scattering policy prevailed, the evil was very conspicuous, and women going about alone felt far less comfortable than under the older system.

There are two ways to explain the fact that, after fifteen years of political experience, the women of Boise voted in large numbers for license and for a policy in handling the red light district which they knew would mean a return to police control. In the first place, it may be said that fifteen years of steady contact with political life had blunted the sensibilities of women and dulled their moral feeling. On the other hand, it may be held that practical experience, under the steady pressure of responsibility, had made them realise the difficulties involved in the handling of these great social problems and had made them feel that a law which could command the support of public opinion, even though it regulated these difficulties, was better than a law which they might consider ideal, but which was incapable of execution.

In Idaho, as in Colorado, the payment of women political workers seems to have become a rather widespread abuse. Under the conditions of the State, with many new settlers constantly arriving, it has long been thought necessary to employ paid workers to register voters, get them out on election-day and influence those who are uncertain. After 1896, women were often hired to do this work, and were paid from three to five dollars a day. With their weak sense of party affiliation, it is claimed that they will work for the party that pays best. A candidate with plenty of money may hire so many workers that it becomes a system of wholesale bribery. It is universally conceded that this is an abuse, and that many women look upon election service as a source of pin money to a degree that is undesirable. Meantime, practical politicians assured me that it was a system the women found in operation when they came in; that far more men than women were paid; and that the abuse could be corrected by proper legislation.

To summarise the matter, we may say that equal suffrage in Idaho has simply accentuated the movement toward setting women free to live their individual lives which general education and participation in industrial life has already carried so far all over the country. Equal suffrage is accepted there, as the higher education of women is accepted in Massachusetts, and the results in the two cases have been much the same.

Surely these reports carry the matter beyond the experimental stage. Conditions in Colourado and Idaho are not identical with those in the East, but they are similar enough to make the experience of these States amount to a demonstration. Meantime the new obligation resting on women is profound. They must learn to "sweat their tempers and learn to know their man." They must become students of public affairs and of institutional life. Old issues are past; and equal suffrage will soon prevail everywhere. Women, like men, have more "rights" in our modern democracies than they can use. Woman's Rights are largely realised; from now on we must front Woman's Duties.

The Modern Family

HE MOST POWERFUL influence in shaping our lives today is the sexual impulse which has created the institution we call the family. Few of us, at least in our modern democracies, live in daily fear that our neighbours will attack and kill us, or carry us off into slavery. Even the hunger for food, that once forced men into action, plays little direct part in the shaping of the lives of most of us. None of those who read these pages would starve if they never did any more work. If they tried to starve, they would be arrested and sent to jail; and if they persisted, they would be fed by force.

Meantime it is sex hunger, manifesting itself in a hundred forms of beauty and ugliness, courtesy and insult, cultivated conversation and ribald jest, beautiful dancing and suggestive indecencies, honour and dishonour, self-repression and prostitution, love and lust, children of gladness and children of shame, that lifts us to such heights as we attain, or plunges us into the hells we create for ourselves. If one could insure one good thing in life for the child one loves, one would ask, not money nor fame, but a continuously happy marriage.

In the past, women have always looked upon marriage and family life as a career; and the majority of men have found their most significant life in the building up of the family institution. Today, however, family life as a career is everywhere called in question. Many women claim to prefer educational opportunity, professional recognition or an independent bank account to husband and children. Social service is exalted; domestic service is debased. Why is it so much nobler to care for other people's children in a social settlement, or in a school, than to care for one's own in a home? Why should women mass themselves together in vast groups as industrial workers, as teachers, as suffragettes? We hear of women's work, of women's careers, of women's clubs, associations and parties, of women's interests, movements, causes. In November 1911, two hundred and twenty women were arrested in London for assaulting the English government in the supposed interest of women. Why do women prefer social to domestic service?

Two reasons spring at once to the mind of any intelligent observer of the life about him. The first is the complexity of our modern life; the second is the nature of the institution of marriage.

A man or woman wishes to live with the one he or she loves. Sexual love is in its very nature restricted, circumscribed, monopolistic — in a word, monogamic. As has been said repeatedly in this volume, the human unit is neither a man nor a woman; it is a man and a woman united in a new personality through the unifying and blending power of love. To say that this unit is exclusive and monogamic is simply saying that it respects its own personality. It can no longer act simply as a man or a woman; it is a family and it must act as such in order to satisfy its own demands. A man can no more act independently of the woman he loves than the heart can act independently of the lungs. The man and woman who compose the new unit are not only flesh of one flesh, but they are one soul, one life; they are a complete organism. And the life of this organism must be persistent to realise its own aims. In all the higher forms of existence, processes move slowly. For nine months a woman carries her baby as a part of her own body; then for three years the father and mother carry the child in their arms; for a score of years they must support, protect and train it before they let it go to seek its own. Hence sexual love must be persistent as well as monogamic.

From all this it follows that each half of the human unit must find the major part of its adult life in devotion to the one it has chosen as its complement. This is no hardship; it is divine opportunity, if love binds the lives in harmonious unity. If love is lacking, then there is no new organism; and such a case falls outside this discussion.

Under the simpler forms of civilisation that have prevailed in the past, it was comparatively easy to find the complement for any particular man or woman. With physical sympathy and desire, little more was needed than common race and the same general social position. With simple personalities even the marriage of convenience was apt to prove happy.

But, today, not only have men become infinitely more complex and self-conscious than formerly, but women have ceased to be a general class; and, in becoming individuals, they have developed wide ranges of individual needs. Instead of fitting at the two or three points of physical desire, race and social position, a man or woman, to live strongly and well in this close union of body and soul, must fit each other at many points. To the older sympathies must be added a common attitude toward religion, education, artistic tastes, social ambitions, industrial aptitudes, and a score of other living sympathies, if the days are to pass in happiness, and each is to maintain his fair share of the life of the new unit. Physical desire still remains the paramount thing, but these other sympathies tend to strengthen it, or their absence may weaken and ultimately destroy it. It is comparatively easy for a person to find a complement to two or three of his, or her, qualities; it is very difficult for a person to find fulfilment for a score of his personal needs in another personality.

In earlier times, too, the individual reached such maturity as he or she was to attain much earlier than now, when education has become a life-long process. Once united, there was comparatively little danger that passing years would develop latent tastes that might prove dissimilar. Today, complete union at twenty may mean many oppositions at forty, if each half of the unit goes on developing its powers. And we must add to this individual complexity and slower development of the present-day men and women the intense self-consciousness of modern times which makes it impossible for us to forget our conditions and go on living in a world once significant and true but now empty or false.

A second cause for the unrest of the present is doubtless to be found in the inflexibility of the institution of the family, under which lovers are allowed to live together and bring into existence the children of their love. The family, as we have it, was shaped under the stress of mediaeval disorder. In such a time men are willing to pay any price for peace and quiet. And so the barbarian invaders, living among the broken fragments of Greek and Roman civilisation, gradually shaped feudalism, culminating in absolute monarchy, which gave them political security. They shaped the Holy Roman Catholic Church that they might worship in peace. They shaped the guilds that they might work quietly, and enjoy the fruits of their labours. The family, with its civil and ecclesiastical sanctions, was formed to protect the personal lives of men and women who wished to live together and rear children.

But with peace, life grew stronger and more intense; and the bonds which the people had shaped, and which had given them security, reached their limits of growth, became painful, and threatened to prevent all further development. The rising cities bought their freedom from feudal lords; even the serfs won better conditions; and the rising national units beat down the older political institutions with their swords. Finally the movements that gather around the French Revolution opened the way for us into the democratic freedom and security which we enjoy today. The guilds were broken up and a measure of freedom was secured, though the industrial institution which shall give us freedom and security in our work is yet to be formed. The Protestant Revolution led us by devious ways into religious freedom where men can worship as they will.

Of all these older institutions, shaped under iron necessity, the only one that remains practically unchanged is the family. Dealing with the most powerful of all our human hungers, as it does, we have not dared to make it fit our modern life. Not only is this true, but the forces of the older state and church which survived, fastened themselves upon this institution and strengthened its resisting power. The church increasingly made marriage into a holy sacrament, so that it not only protected lovers, but became a subtle, inviolable and indissoluble mystery. The state sanctioned the family, and made it an instrument for regulating political and property rights. Formal society proclaimed the family and made it the standard for respectability.

Two centuries hence, our family, with its sacramental significances, its lack of a eugenic conscience, its financial subordination of women, its frequent lack of love and sympathy, its primogeniture, and its determining power over social opportunity, will be as incomprehensible to students of institutional forms as the Holy Roman Empire is to us today. Who will then understand how church and state could have licensed and consummated marriages between young and inexperienced people, marriages which were to be binding on their thought, feeling and action for life without requiring some time, however brief, between the application for a license and the final binding of vows? Who will be able to understand how church and state could have sanctioned marriage between a broken-down old noble and a young and inexperienced girl of seventeen? How will the future student explain the fact that in New Jersey state and church combined to sanction and bless the marriage of an imbecile woman and of her offspring until they had produced 148 feeble-minded children to curse the state.**50**

Who will then understand why a man and woman who had not only ceased to love each other but had come to feel a deep repugnance for each other should have been compelled to share bed and board, even when there were no children, until even murder seemed preferable to such slavery of soul and body? How can this student understand woman's economic dependence, her uncertain income, her insecure rights in property for which she toiled side by side with her husband? Who will then believe that in the year 1911 an English citizen could go before a court and secure an order for legalised rape, under the name of restitution of marital rights?

Meantime every issue of the daily press counts as its choicest items stories of the shameful and soul-destroying ways in which men and women are trying to live their lives in spite of this medieval institution. So far-reaching is the unrest, that at each new revelation of marital heresy, society feels constrained to rush forward and frantically denounce the heretic in order to prove its own orthodoxy.

Our own attitude toward marriage as a sacrament to be directed by a church, or as a pleasure to be exploited by individuals, must be changed if the life of the family is to be re-established as the great vocation of earnest men and women. Intelligence must be turned upon this problem as upon all others that vitally affect our lives. What President Eliot has called "the conspiracy of silence touching matters of sex" must be broken, and when it is, I believe honest men will agree with Ellen Key that "In love humanity has found the form of selection most conducive to the ennoblement of the species."**51**

In this field, at least, a eugenic conscience must take the place of the older theological conscience.**52** We must recognise the infamy of knowingly bringing defective children into existence. We must agree that under no conditions should people tainted with syphilis be allowed to marry; and that those subject to imbecility or insanity should not be allowed to live together unless they are unsexed.**53** Justice to future generations, and protection of the state, demands at least this much.

Whether alcoholics, those suffering from congenital sense defects, and near relatives, should be allowed to marry may still be an open question; but it should be recognised that the state has the right and the duty to inquire into these conditions and to impose restrictions. Society must come to feel that it is at least as shameful for a broken old noble to live with a young girl under the forms of marriage as for two young lovers to live together outside them.

As to what the personal, social and industrial relation of man and wife should be, we have widely different views and practices. The older view, still embodied in the practice of most nations, and best seen in Germany and England, is that the woman's duty is to complement the husband. He does what he wishes, so far as he can, and the wife rounds out the whole. It is the old ideal of later savagery, that the man should provide and protect, and the woman should breed children, care for the home, pray and wait.

This is really the same ideal that dominated our political life until a hundred and fifty years ago. It was the duty of the lords to direct and fight; the peasants should work and wait. In politics there gradually grew up a middle class which combined with the peasants to overthrow the older privileges; and now all classes direct, fight, wait and watch together. Whether this democratic idea is finally to prevail, we may not know; but it is well worth trying, and the results so far are full of promise.

In the same way, in the family, a great middle class of wives has grown up, largely since 1870, through education and industry, as the burgers did in political life, and these emancipated women are insisting that the peasant of the family, the *Hausfrau*, shall join with them and dethrone the husband so that all shall share life's responsibilities together as free and equal partners. In fact, in America, the revolution has already come; and, as in the earlier stages of political revolutions, those deposed are having a hard time to maintain even their equal share of opportunity.

But the parallel between political and domestic life is not complete, and if pushed too far the analogy is mischievous. The assumption of physical, intellectual and social superiority on the side of political lords and domestic lords was the same. It is possible, however, rightly or wrongly, to reduce all the people to the same political level and set them all at work doing the same things. But between men and women there was not only the assumption of physical and mental difference, but there was and must always be the infinite difference of sex. In domestic life, the women cannot live without men nor the men without women. Not only would the generations fail, but the present generation would lose its deepest meaning, if either sex were banished or debased.

In their reactions against old abuses, writers like Mrs Gilman or Olive Schreiner try to create a world for women alone, on the political analogy. Men might be tolerated as fathers; but, to secure political freedom, these leaders would turn to that nebulous creation of social reformers, the state; and it should subsidise the mothers in their periods of need. But there are only two ingredients out of which a nation can be formed: one is women; the other is men. Shall woman in her time of need turn to a state made up of other women, or to a state made up of men? Obviously it must be to both; and if woman is to depend on men, she might as well depend on man. No, in the political revolutions we broke up artificial, outworn and unjust combinations; but in this domestic revolution we are breaking up and must readjust the fundamental unit of life.

Men and women must live and work together in the domestic unit, and they cannot do the same things. Nature has specialised their functions and each must supplement the other. Even in Germany, the *Hausfrau* is not going back to an exclusive service of children, cooking and church; nor in America will man continue to be merely the breadwinner and the father of children. With the enlightenment that is on the way, we shall see that husband and wife can have no antagonistic differences. Each profits in all that really benefits the other; and slowly we shall shape a new institution based on absolute equality, and at the same time on complementary service.

In this adjustment, legal forms can help or hinder; but they cannot prevent nor compel the final action of human beings. Sex instinct is stronger than any human law. The law can, however, help us in regulating conditions of marriage, in settling disputes about common property and children, and in determining how the contract may be set aside when that becomes necessary.

The right of the church to sanction or regulate the family, rests in a belief that marriage involves spiritual changes and obligations that make it a sacrament, in its nature inviolable, and to be administered only by the church, like the sacrament of baptism. This is a belief resting not in eugenic considerations, nor in the human needs of the persons involved, but in theological dogmas with which this chapter cannot deal. Hence we shall maintain that the church has no more right to control matters of marriage than it has to interfere in business or political relations.

The state, on the other hand, meaning by the state the whole community, must concern itself with the marriage of its individuals. The commonwealth must have future citizens, and these should be strong and intelligent; hence it must prevent the breeding of the unfit. If parents die, or fail in obligations, the community must care for the children. In case of disagreement between married people, the courts of the community must settle disputes about children and property; hence the state must know when a man and woman determine to live together. The regulation of marriage certainly belongs to the state, that is, to all of us.

Marriage should therefore always be a matter of definite and open record in the archives of the community. It should also be advertised, through the public record, for a considerable time, preferably six months or a year, before consummation, that the past experiences of contracting parties may be looked up by interested friends or officials, and the marriage of the unfit prevented; and so that mere caprice and passion shall have time to realise their mistake and turn away. The form which the final ceremony of marriage will take can well be left to the tastes and traditions of the contracting parties.

The question of rights in children, or in property acquired after marriage, should be settled by the state; and it is hard to see how it can ever be settled satisfactorily except on a basis of equal partnership No man should be contented with a woman to bear and train his children, and create a social atmosphere for his home, who is not worth half of what he makes; and the same holds true of a woman. So with regard to children, while one parent or the other may, under certain conditions, be given the direction of the child's life, it is hard to imagine any circumstances that would justify society in refusing either father or mother the right frequently to see his child.

Since marriages must be contracted in youth and since inexperienced people must make mistakes and the wisest must sometimes change, it will sometimes happen that men and women must face the possibility of separation. The problem of divorce is very difficult.**54** In less than twenty years, from 1887 to 1906, 945,625 divorces were granted in the United States; so that probably today there are nearly one million divorced people in this country. Generally speaking, the divorce rate increases as one goes westward. In 1900, the State of Washington led the country with 184 divorces for each 100,000 of population. For the whole country we averaged 73 per 100,000 of population. Japan alone leads us with 215, while England and Wales had only 2. England grants divorce only for infidelity; and on the man's side it must be accompanied by cruelty; all divorce cases must be tried in London, and the expense, never less than two hundred dollars, is prohibitive for the poor. Meantime, England grants many separation orders; and it seems sure that the Royal Commission, which has been taking evidence for the past three years, will favour a freer system of divorce.

While divorce is increasing steadily all over the world, and most rapidly in the most intelligent and progressive sections, the subject is so bound up with our most deep-seated prejudices that it is difficult to secure any intelligent thinking on the subject. Thus, most people think Sioux Falls, in South Dakota, and Reno, Nevada, are places of free divorce, but the fact is that twenty-one other States have a higher divorce rate than South Dakota; and fourteen have a higher rate than Nevada. So, too, the impression that divorces spring from hasty action is certainly wrong, for in 46.5 per cent of those for which we have records there had been a separation of more than three years before the divorce was granted. The idea that people generally seek divorces that they may marry some one else seems also unfounded, since in the cases for which we have records, less than forty per cent remarry within a year.

There are three main objections which one hears urged against free divorce. The first is that organised society rests on the family, and with free divorce anarchy would ensue. In reply, it is pointed out that the same argument was used to support kings, aristocracies and a universal church. All these have been set aside, in many parts of the earth, and society seems even more stable than before. The love of men and women is probably more powerful and less in need of adventitious support than either patriotism or religion.

In the second place, it is claimed that children will suffer when parents separate. It is replied that this is true, but they were already suffering when parents had ceased to love each other. The fact that children are involved in only two out of five divorces seems to indicate that children hold parents together when the opposition is not too strong; and when a separation occurs, those who favour divorce claim that a child is better off with either father or mother alone than with both if love is absent.

In the third place, it is pointed out that often only one desires the divorce and that this brings tragedy to the other life. In reply it is claimed that many of the tragedies of life have always gathered around the love of men and women, that when marriage is declined tragedy often follows, and that compelling a person to live with some one whom he does not love, and may even dislike, is more tragic than any separation.

In conclusion, advocates of free divorce claim that their proposals are profoundly conservative, that they are seeking to bring marriage back to its eternally binding realities. They say that under our present conditions of restricted divorce, we have widespread prostitution, constant irregularities that are tolerated and condoned, and a million divorced people, some prevented from remarrying and all socially ostracised, so that the whole group is a dangerous element in our midst. These advocates claim that with free divorce, granted some months after the determination to separate had been registered in the public records, the love of men and women and their mutual love for their children would be free to bind families together in permanent trust and open honesty; and that with all excuse for irregularity absent, the unfaithful man or woman would sink to the level of unfaithfulness in business or political life. With freedom to readjust their lives, if they preferred to keep what they had and get what they could, they would simply take their place among thieves and liars, and most of them would disappear.

All transitions are hard, and this one in which we are involved is most difficult of all; but no one can study the conditions around him without seeing that change is inevitable and that we are not going back to our earlier ideals. At the same time, no one can read the singularly scholarly and fair-minded presentations of Ellen Key**55** without feeling that she has a vision of the future.

With regard to the nature of the material plant in which the family should live, there are also two widely different ideals struggling for favour in the public mind, and for realisation in practice. The one ideal, while recognising the changes necessitated by modern conditions, would still seek to retain those features which have been supposed to make for family privacy, the kitchen, the nursery, and the garden. The other would frankly accept our changed conditions, and pass on to the larger groups of socialised buildings, with common kitchens, day nurseries, and parks.**56**

This question has been discussed in the chapter on industry, and it will be considered again in the following chapter. Meantime there can be no doubt that love is reticent so far as the outside world is concerned; and domesticity must always demand a large measure of privacy. It still remains to be proved that this can be secured, in the absence of a private kitchen, nursery and garden. Children, too, seem to need the personal care and constant love of mothers, and women seem to need a long period of loving and caring for a family to round out a deeply significant life.

To summarise this chapter we may say that the realisation of romantic love, under conditions of domesticity, is necessary for men and women, and for the well-being of the race. Our present marriage system is defective, and needs to be corrected through the creation of a eugenic conscience. It should be taken out of the hands of the church and made more difficult by the state. Women's property rights should be defined and safeguarded, and men and women should never live together when they are repugnant to each other.

Family Life as a Vocation

HE GREATEST OF all wisdom is that which leads men and women to see the real significance of their lives while they are still living. Life's values, like the manna in the wilderness, must be gathered daily. If not nourished day by day the power to live atrophies and dies; and no one can live well today on the shrunken memories of yesterday. A full and significant life is its own justification; and in a last analysis philosophies and theologies offer us only the life more abundantly which the great Teacher said he came into the world to bring. Buddhism offers us eternal peaceful existence in Nirvana; Epicureanism offers pleasure, which is but an intensification of life; Stoicism offers us life freed from disturbing forces; and the great lure which Christianity has always held before humanity is life eternal. Life is its own justification.

We have maintained throughout this volume that complete self-realisation is impossible for the half-units which we call men and women, when either lives alone. On every side of their natures they are complementary; and the unit of human life must be found in the family composed of a man and woman who love each other and the children born of their love. "There are two worlds below, the home and outside of it." It is in this unit, under the stress of sexual passion and maternal love, that all the finer forces of our civilisation have had their origin. Unselfishness, devotion, pity and the higher altruisms all hark back to the home as their source.

But, meantime, evil counsels prevail and one hears everywhere of the antagonistic interests of men and women. There can be no real rivalry between a man's soul and his body, between science and religion, between man and woman. The trouble all rests back in the failure to realise the incompleteness of man or woman alone for any of the purposes of life. And there is that evil notion which still afflicts economics that when two trade one must lose. The fact is that, in all honest trade, buyer and seller gain alike; and fair exchange makes all who participate in it rich. It is so in all real relations between these half-creatures we call men and women. In agreement, association and cooperation lies strong and significant life for both. In antagonism, separation and competition lie arid, poor, mean lives, egotistic and conceited, vapid and fickle.

In primitive life, the family furnished a full and adequate career for men and women alike. The political life was the family life; each family was a religious group; families mustered for war; and each family maintained within itself a wide range of industrial activity. But, because this unit was so basal, because all later special developments of state, church and industry came from it, it was steadily perverted. Warped from its original purpose, it has served in turn, as we have seen, to define and secure all our later institutions until it has become the servant of state, church, social ambition, property and industrial advance. Marriage and the birthrate are seldom discussed today from the point of view of individual needs; but are almost always considered from the point of view of national and industrial efficiencies.

Today men and women are confronted by two tempters which constantly lure them away from the complete living of the family; one is work, and the other is comfort. With the majority of people in our modern industrial democracies work uses up the hours and the energy of life. We have passed into a time when our habitual material needs are great, and the products of work are shamelessly diverted to the excessive uses of comparatively few individuals and groups. Hence millions of workers march along the narrow dark roads that lead through factories and farms to the grave. Only little patches of their nervous systems are ever used, but all their energy flows through these sections day after day, leaving their lives dull and empty.

Marriage for these workers means decreased earning power for the woman, with increased needs for the family, especially when the children come. As one watches the procession of young factory and shop women, with Sunday finery and some leisure, passing over into draggled factory mothers, with no finery and no leisure, one marvels at the strength of the forces with which nature drives them to their destiny. And yet, even with these hopeless workers, marriage and children mark the heights of life.

With others, who are economically freer, work has become an obsession. A Charles Darwin or a Herbert Spencer turns all of life's forces to shaping facts into science; our industrial leaders mint their hours into dollars; our reformers give up their lives that social conditions may be changed; our society leaders trade life for triumphs. Meantime we all know, or would know if we stopped to consider, that we are here to live life fully and significantly day by day. But domesticity takes time and effort, and so the hurrying specialist follows the narrow line of success until he or she becomes a machine for manufacturing generalisations, for painting pictures, for performing surgical operations or for merely getting money. The richest woman in America said with approval recently that her son was too busy to fall in love.

As industry drives the mass of workers and specialists away from life's deepest realisations, so the desire to become comfortable, physically and mentally, through avoiding the deeper experiences of life, robs many of those who have a large measure of economic freedom. In all periods of great wealth this disease of ease has afflicted mankind. Life more abundantly comes only at the price of vigorous living; and love travels always in company with anxiety. It would be well, says Cicero, to have children, were it not for the fear of losing them. Let a man apply this principle to wife, friends, possessions and enthusiasm in general and life sinks into utter worthlessness.

The love of ease among women is in a measure independent of the emancipation movement, but the entry of great numbers of young women into lines of independent livelihood has placed them in a condition where the ideals of a materialistic and commercial civilisation appeal to them with great force. Many of them have been liberally educated and are living lives of independence. They lodge in flats or boarding houses where they have no responsibilities for the routine work connected with daily living. They carry their own latch-keys; and no one interferes with their friendships or their pleasures. They read the books they like, attend the theatres that appeal to them, and avoid people who bore them. One can easily understand why these young women hesitate before abandoning their easy conditions for the uncertain economic position of wife and mother, with a man whose career lies in the future. And yet here, as everywhere, one must lose one's life to gain it.

What then does daily association of a man and woman who belong together do for them? It gives gladness and peace, and these are fundamental conditions for all good and healthful living. It gives incentive to effort, for a man or woman dares not fail before the one he or she loves; but, in case of failure, it gives comfort and support, for love understands and credits intent and effort as highly as achievement. It complements the powers, for it gives four eyes, four hands and two minds with but one aim. And in this it does not simply multiply by two, but the blended powers are far more than two times one. It calls into activity all the gracious, artistic and altruistic powers of the soul. Surely these are gifts for which we may well forego some material comforts, may well work, and even face anxieties unafraid.

Each part of the human unit must educate the other to a realisation of the fullness of life. This education is not entirely dependent on physical intimacy. It is the development of soul and spirit. It polishes the manners, cultivates the voice, broadens the judgements, sharpens the wit. It makes conversation an art and discussion significant. A woman-hating man or a man-hating woman is an unpolished and half-alive creature, whether he be a mediaeval saint, or she a militant suffragette, or they both be simply commonplace egoists.

Because married life is so perfect when it finds its highest levels, it is capable of sinking to any form of vulgarity, base betrayal and cynicism when realisation fails. The God to whom noblest souls aspire in hours of deepest exaltation, is the God invoked by the ribald drunkard when he curses his comrade. The family life we are discussing is the subject of most of the vulgar and indecent jokes of the disappointed and the unfit. The earth which nourishes the nations, merely soils the boots of the boor who unthinkingly lives on her bounty.

On the working side the life of the family has an evil record for pettiness and monotony, but much of this is due to wrong comparisons. A woman who does her own housework would presumably have to work in any case. Is the work of the family more petty or monotonous than the work of the factory, shop or office? Surely the woman who spends her days looking after the details of furnishing a house and keeping it clean, of providing and serving meals, of looking after clothing and caring for children, has a world of self-expression compared with which factory and shop work is infinitely petty and mean. In the social life of friends, neighbourhood, school and church she is at least as well placed as the factory worker. If the woman has the preparation required for teaching or independent business, she will find ways to use her powers that will relieve the routine of housework. And if the family has means to hire help, the wife has a position from which she can exercise social and political power superior to that of the foot-loose celibate.

Meantime, the housework grows steadily simpler and less exacting, even with the growing complexity of our modern life. Most of the primitive industries have left the home, and products come from the factory ready to use. Furnace heating, hot and cold water, improved cooking conditions and many domestic inventions of our day are keeping housework well abreast of other unspecialised work in attractiveness.

The fact that domestic servants are scarce and unwilling to do general housework, in no way disproves the soundness of these conclusions. The wife, if she is a real wife, and we are discussing no others, is working for those she loves, under conditions of free initiative. The general servant is working for those who will not even admit her right to participate in their social life, and instead of freedom in her industrial life, she must generally adjust her efforts to the caprices of an untrained mistress. Well-trained mistresses, who know how to work themselves and who have a democratic sense of human values, seldom have trouble in securing able servants, even in this transition time when the shops and factories are calling so loudly to working girls.

No intelligence which a woman may possess needs remain unused in the handling of a family. Women spend most of the household money today, at least in lower and middle-class homes. To use wisely the family pay-envelope requires knowledge and judgement of a high order. Problems in economics, sanitation, food-values and aesthetics confront the housewife at every turn of the day's work. "Even a slave need not work as a slave;" and a woman living with the man she loves is the freest woman on earth, so far as mind and spirit are concerned.

But the factory girl, or the teacher, or the professional woman who seeks the fulfilment of all of life in the factory, the school or the consulting-room, will soon tire and clamour for relief. The housewife, or the mistress of a home, must likewise seek life away from her work if she is to love it and wake each morning with a desire to continue it. Luckily we have reached a place where working women in the home are seeking supplementary life outside, and they seem to be quite as successful in their search as are factory girls or teachers.

To the man, family life, of the kind we are considering, brings a vital connection with the past and the future. Reputation, possessions, friends, all become deeply significant when a man becomes a link in the generations of men. In establishing his material home, and modifying it to the changing conditions of the family; in building up a social setting for the group; in projecting his work and his service into the future, he is held to highest standards by the fact that he is working with the partner of his choice, and for interests that are in harmony with the constitution of the universe.

Of the greater physical health of married people there can be no doubt. Statistics all show the greater longevity of married people, and insurance companies recognise it. The celibate type of physical degeneration is so well differentiated that it can generally be recognised even among strangers, at least after forty.**57** On the moral side, too, very few criminals are found among married people.

If children come to bless these homes of men and women, then even intellectual life may shift to a higher level than was before possible. With advancing years intellectual interests tend to become specialised. The man or woman gives up singing, ceases to be interested in plant life, stops reading poetry. One activity after another is cut off and interests concentrate in some comparatively small field of work or pleasure. But when a child comes, the parents are forced to start over the round of human interests and thought once more. Before, they lived it as children; now, they live the cycle as grown men and women.

No matter how completely a woman has given up music, she will some day find herself singing when she holds her baby in her arms. As she recites Mother Goose and the fairy and folk-lore tales, she moves through the path of man's upward progress, led by a child, but with the life and understanding of adult years. As she walks with her child in the garden and in the fields, she is driven to a new interpretation of the world of nature. Few things can so broaden, quicken and enrich the intellectual life as growing up with one's children.

On the social side, a parent who has children is forced to live in all the social world around him. The water supply, the sewage, pure foods, vacant lots, paving, fast driving in the streets, police protection, undesirable residents, saloons and churches, schools and libraries — everything that touches the social well-being — touches him vitally and imperatively. The foot-loose celibate can always go away. The parent finds it difficult to leave the place where he has planted his roof-tree. Of course, there are many unmarried people, and people who are childless, who live this domestic life vicariously through friends or other people's children. One cannot but be grateful that life is so organised that no woman can be entirely shut off, unless she wills it, from the fructifying life that knits together the generations of the old and the young.

Ideals are very powerful in determining conduct, and the ideals of extreme individualism, now so constantly presented by certain leaders among emancipated women, must bear bitter fruit for an army of women in the future. While the women are young, ambition and the charm of freedom bear them gaily along. Generally better educated than the men of their own class, habituated to a personal expenditure which would correspond with a large family expenditure, their intelligence prevents their falling desperately in love with the men whom they might marry. But in the thirties they have visions of the future which are deeply disturbing; and in the forties they face the tragedy of a lonely old age. Some men and women there must always be whose lives lack the fulfilment of family life because of ill health or the accidents of personal relations. But most women, if they are willing to pay the same price for a significant family life that they so gladly pay for professional success, will find the way open to live all of life. Why is it that women count it an honour to work and starve for an art, but dishonour to undergo privations for their children? All that is here said of women may be said of men, but the man's period of family life is longer than woman's, and the tragedy of lonely old age with him seems less overwhelming.

The old plea that we must have an army of celibate women because in civilised countries there is a preponderance of females does not hold at present in the United States. The census of 1910 shows an excess of 2,691,678 males in this country. Nor is this entirely due to immigration. More boys than girls are always born in civilised lands; and of native white people born of native parents in the United States there were, in 1910, 25,229,294 males and 24,259,147 females, a difference obviously due to natural causes. New England alone in America has a preponderance of females; and the excess there, as also in England and Germany, is needed all along the frontiers of civilisation. With the industrial and social freeing of women now going on, we may reasonably hope that the communities of old maids left behind, through the emigration of young men, will be broken up

Of course, it will be pointed out that many men and women

who do marry fail to realise the ideal presented in these pages. Every form of living is dangerous and not every one can hope to be a successful husband and father or wife and mother. Even devotion to religion furnishes many inmates for insane asylums; athletic contests leave a line of cripples behind them; and railroad disasters fill thousands of graves annually. The institution of marriage has had no such intelligence applied to its improvement during the past years as has been given to perfecting railroads; and since founding a family is a more difficult undertaking than making a journey, one need not be astonished at the number of fatalities. Even if the institution of marriage were as intelligently and carefully brought up to date as railroad systems are, it would still remain dangerous to live either in or out of marriage.

And yet the danger could be greatly reduced by proper education of youth. At present we are educating 10,000,000 girls in the state schools of America, and as many boys. They are spending eight to twelve years, under the direction of celibate women teachers, sharpening their intelligence. Their most important work in life is to be the making of homes, but they are supposed to master this art through imitating the homes in which they grow up Many of these are unworthy of imitation, and they are all in process of transition.

Every girl should be thoroughly trained in handling an income and in spending money wisely. She should have a general knowledge of household sanitation, of water supply and sewage, of foods and their preparation. She should know about clothes, their cost, wearing qualities and decorative values. She should have a sense of the family and its significance in life; of at least the social relations that husband and wife must maintain toward each other if their partnership is to be happy and effective. She should have the beginnings of a eugenic conscience established in her, and she should know something of the care of infancy. All this should be given in the school, if it is not definitely given in the home, and no girl who goes through the eighth grade should escape it. Before the girl is married, she should have wise counsel from mature women who have lived and learned the art of living. Boys should, of course, also be trained in comparable directions for this great part of their lives.

Something is already being done in this direction through the establishing of special courses in domestic science, and allied branches in our schools. The fact that educational leaders are awake to the need was shown by the applause that followed Superintendent Harvey's plea for this training in his paper on the education of girls at the Superintendents' Association in St Louis in February, 1912.**58** The leading educators of the country greeted his plea with an enthusiasm called out by no other paper of the session.

Every woman, then, and every man, not debarred by disease or accident and not specially dedicated to a work which precludes marriage, should spend his life in a family group, not that the state may have more soldiers, or factory employees, but that he may realise the deepest significance of his life. In this life the woman should be as free as the man, an equal financial partner, and should share in all the social and political opportunities of the community. When she bears children, she should have special protection, support and reverence; and support should come from the father of her children. If he fails her, then the group, in its capacity as a state, should care for her honourably. But to justify this protection and reverence, she should bring to her special functions as mother of the generations a strong body, an intelligent mind, a eugenic conscience and an absolute devotion to the children born of her love.

Conclusion

HE LAST TWO hundred years have revolutionised nearly all of our deepest conceptions concerning the relations of human beings to religion, government, property, and to each other. New knowledge has given us partial control over vast forces of nature; and has so increased our mobility as almost to free us from limitations of space. We have had wonderful visions of the possibilities that lie in intelligent human cooperation, and have begun to realise them in a hundred new forms. In the midst of these compelling changes, women could no more remain undisturbed, within the confines of kitchen and nursery, than men could remain on their little New England farms or cobbling shoes and making tin pans in the petty workshops of a century ago. But meantime the special interests of women have been sadly confused because of the larger changes in which all human relations have been involved in this time of readjustment. Instead of talking of unquiet women today, we should talk of an unquiet world.

In the midst of this confusion, most of those who have sought to secure a truer relation of women to the life around them have worked on the lines of minimising sex differences. It has been felt that the educational, industrial, social and political limitations under which women rested were due to the desire of men to exploit them. Men, being free, had developed for themselves an ideal world of thought and work; and if women wished to be free and happy, they needed only to break down the barriers separating them from this man's world.

Most of these barriers are now down; but the women who study in universities, teach in the schools, maintain offices as doctors or lawyers, collect news for the press, tend spindles in a factory or sell ribbons at a counter have found that the man's world is far from ideal and that by entering it they have not escaped the special limitations of their sex. Everywhere the feeling is abroad that, instead of having arrived at a destination, women have embarked on a journey fraught with many uncertainties.

This volume has been written in the belief that men and women alike will achieve greatest freedom and happiness, not by minimising sex differences, but by frankly recognising them and using them. If we could reduce men and women to sameness, we should destroy at least half the values of human life. They are not alike; but they are perfectly supplementary. The unit can never be a man, nor a woman; it must always be a man and a woman. This means that in all the activities essential to human development men and women must carefully study to find what each can best provide.

Thus we must some day have a Church, not composed exclusively of male priests and women worshipers, not confined to rationalistic appeal, nor to ritualistic observance, but expressing the whole range of human aspiration toward the unknown. Rational men and women of feeling must combine with reverent men and intelligent women to create a belief and a service which will express all the longings of humanity toward perfection.

So in government, we must have a state which will be not only just but merciful; which will concern itself not only with militant economics but also with human well-being. If men are more capable in expressing the katabolic needs of aggression and protection, women must furnish the anabolic products of care and conservation. If women must help pay the bills and nurse the wounded, they must first have a voice in determining whether there shall be a war. Men and women must join their qualities in building and caring for cities, and in shaping nations, where they can both live their largest lives.

In education, we must devise institutions which will provide for the special needs of women; and we must have the combined qualities of men and women brought to bear on children of both sexes, and at all ages. The foster parents of the nation's children must be both men and women. The present attempt to exploit our twenty millions of boys and girls in the interest of a sex will be a crime against humanity when we are intelligent enough to see its real meaning.

The specialisation going on in industry means infinite variety if we look at the whole field of activity. Some parts of the world's work are specially fitted for men; other parts to women. No intelligent division of labour has been attempted in the period since all work was transformed by our modern inventions. Possibly men should do most of the dressmaking, and women should make men's clothing, but no intelligent man or woman can doubt that most work falls naturally into the hands of one sex or the other. Some day we shall know enough so that there will be little or no industrial competition between men and women.

It is, however, in the family that both men and women must find their deepest supplementary values. Sex antagonism can do much to impoverish and ruin individual lives; but the monogamic and persistent union of lovers, surrounded by their children, will easily survive all the mistakes of a time of transition. In the meantime, those who would uphold the finest family ideals of the past have less cause to fear the militant agitator than they have to fear the idle, parasitic wife, who relies on her legal rights to give her luxuries without labour, position without leadership, and wifehood without the care and responsibility of children.

From the point of view of this book, all the efforts to open the doors of opportunity, through which women can pass into the man's world, are but preparations for the beginning of a journey. The sooner all such doors are opened the better, for then a great source of dangerous sex antagonism will pass away; and the energy of reformers will be set free to work out the difficult problem of supplementary sex adjustments.

And meantime, sex remains the greatest mystery and the most powerful thing in human life. Its deeper values are lost sight of when men and women are warring over work, wages, and votes, just as the meaning of religion has been lost when priests and laity sought to advance their meanly selfish interests. But in the crises of life it always comes back. When a great ship founders in midocean, and but a third of the people can be saved, there is then no question of woman's rights. In the darkness of early morning, eager men's hands place their women in the life-boats and push them off. The poorest peasant woman takes precedence over any man. Almost every woman there would prefer to stay and die with her man; would glory in staying and dying if he might thus be saved; but in her keeping are the generations of the future, and she is weak, therefore the strong gladly stand back and go down to death. The solution of woman's place in the society of the future must be based on a recognition of the supplementary forces.

Notes & References

1) The fact that sexual selection does not play the part in organic evolution which Darwin assigned it does not affect this statement. See chapter on Sexual Selection in Yves Delagee and Marie Goldsmith, *The Theories of Evolution*, New York: Huebsch, 1912.

2) Helen B Thompson, *Psychological Norms in Men and Women*, University of Chicago Press, 1903, p 167.

3) William I Thomas, *Sex and Society*, University of Chicago Press, 1907, p 21.

4) Karl Pearson denies this. See *The Chances of Death*, London, 1897, Vol I, p 256.

5) C W Saleeby in *Woman and Womanhood*, New York: Mitchell Kennerley, 1911, p 54, maintains that woman is biologically more variable than man, and that woman's less variable activity is due to her training.

6) Patrick Geddes and Arthur Thompson, in *The Evolution of Sex*, D Appleton & Co, 1889, first advanced this position.

7) C W Saleeby, *Woman and Womanhood*, New York: Mitchell Kennerley, 1911, Ch V.

8) Marshall, *Journal of Anatomy and Physiology*, July 1892.

9) Havelock Ellis, *Man and Woman*, Contemporary Science Series, p 97.

10) Helen Bradford Thompson, *Psychological Norms in Men and Women*, University of Chicago Press, 1903, p 171.

11) Ellen Kay, *Love and Ethics*, New York: Huebsch, 1911, p 52.

12) Helen B Thompson, *Psychological Norms in Men and Women*, University of Chicago Press, 1903, p 171.

13) See chapter on Periodicity in G Stanley Hall, *Adolescence*,

Vol I, p 472.

14) Karin Michaelis, *The Dangerous Age,* John Lane Co, 1911, is said to have sold 80,000 in six weeks when it first appeared in Berlin. *The Bride of the Mistletoe,* by James Lane Allen (Macmillan), deals with the same period.

15) William I Thomas, *Sex and Society,* University of Chicago Press, 1907, p 149. Ellen Kay, in *Love and Marriage,* G P Putnam's Sons, 1911, traces the same lines of growth.

16) *Proverbs* XXXI:10.

17) T G Tucker, *Life in Ancient Athens,* Macmillan Co, 1906, Ch VIII.

18) Olive Schreiner, *Woman and Labour,* New York: Frederick A Stokes Co, 1911, chapters on Parasitism.

19) James Donaldson, *Woman: Her Position and Influence in Ancient Greece and Rome and Among the Early Christians,* Longmans, Green, and Co, 1907.

20) R de Maulde la Claviere, *The Woman of the Renaissance. A Study in Feminism,* translated by George H Ely, New York: G P Putnam's Sons, 1900.

21) *The Highway,* London, November 1911.

22) Helen R Olin, *The Women of a State University,* G P Putnam's Sons, 1909.

23) Marion Talbot, *The Education of Women,* University of Chicago Press, 1910.

24) *Report of the United States Commissioner of Education,* 1910, p 132.

25) Eight hundred and eighty-one Harvard graduates, twenty-five years after graduation, had but 1,226 children. If half were boys, we have but 613 sons for 881 Harvard graduates. Hugo Münsterberg, *The Americans* Boston: Houghton, Mifflin & Co, 1901, p 582.

26) See chapter on Education of Adolescent Girls, in G Stanley Hall, *Adolescence,* New York: D Appleton & Co, 1904.

27) Rheta Childe Dorr, *What Eight Million Women Want,* Boston: Small, Maynard & Co, 1910.

28) W A Newman Dorland, *The Age of Mental Virility.* New York:

The Century Company, 1908.

29) See Hugo Münsterberg, *The Americans*, pp 558-89, Boston: Houghton, Mifflin & Co, 1901.

30) *Report of the United States Commissioner of Education*, 1910, Vol II, p 1139.

31) W L Courtney, *The Feminine Note in Fiction*, London: Chapman & Hall, 1904; the author tries to prove that there is such a thing as a feminine style in fiction.

32) Charlotte Perkins Gilman, *Woman and Economics*, Boston: Small, Maynard & Co, 1898. See also Olive Schreiner, New York: Frederick A Stokes Co, 1911.

33) The Supreme Court of the United States, in passing on the "Oregon laundry case," in 1907, declared a bill limiting a woman's working hours constitutional. See the *Brief for the State of Oregon*, prepared by Louis D Brandeis, published by The National Consumers' League, 105 East 22nd Street, New York.

34) Dudley, *Principles and Practices of Gynaecology*, pp 23-24, says that among Indian women want of care during and after labour leads to numberless evils.

35) Edith Abbott, *Women in Industry: A Study in American Economic History*, New York: D Appleton & Co, 1910.

36) Earl Barnes, Children's Ideals, in *Studies in Education*, Vol II, p 237; also School Girls' Ideas of Women's Occupations by Sarah Young, in *Studies in Education*, Vol II, p 259.

37) C Hanford Henderson, *Pay-Day*, Boston: Houghton, Mifflin Co, 1911.

38) See the recent volume, based on investigations made by the National Consumers' League, *Making Both Ends Meet* by Sue Ainslie Clark and Edith Wyatt, The Macmillan Co, 1911. See, also, *Saleswomen in Mercantile Stores* by Elizabeth Beardsley Butler, published by the Charities Publication Committee, for the Russell Sage Foundation, 1912.

39) Madame Gnauck Kühne, *Die Deutsche Frau*.

40) B L Hutchins, Woman's Industrial Career in *The Sociological Review*, October 1909.

41) Dr Ethel Vaughan-Sawyer, speaking before the Fabian

Women's Group, in 1910, said: "Fortunately, after the first two or three months, most children will thrive equally well when artificially fed, so long as the milk is good and reliable, and is properly prepared." All of our facts go to disprove this statement.

42) Pamphlet entitled *Report on Industrial Employment of Married Women and Infant Mortality*, signed by Dr John Robertson, the Medical Officer of Health, Birmingham.

43) Earl Barnes, *Studies in Education*, Philadelphia, 1902, Vol II, pp 5-80.

44) Jane Addams, *Democracy*, New York: The Macmillan Co, 1902, p 221.

45) *The History of Woman Suffrage*, by Elizabeth Cady Stanton, Susan B Anthony and Ida Husted Harper, Rochester, NY, 4 volumes.

46) Seventeen Hundred Rural Vote-Sellers, by A Z Blair, *McClure's Magazine*, November 1911.

47) Bertha Rembaugh, *The Political Status of Women in the United States*, G P Putnam's Sons, 1912, gives complete information to date.

48) Helen L Sumner, *Equal Suffrage. The Results of an Investigation Made in Colorado for the Collegiate Equal Suffrage League of New York State.* New York: Harper & Bros, 1909.

49) Mr Lawrence Lewis, in the *Outlook* for January 27 1906, analyses the election returns for parts of Pueblo City and vicinity, and he finds from 25 to 46 per cent of the vote was cast by women, and the proportion of women increased with the intelligence and *morale* of the precinct.

50) See *The Kalikak Family*, by Herbert H Goddard, New York: Macmillan Company, 1912.

51) Ellen Key, *Love and Marriage*, New York: G P Putnam's Sons, 1911

52) See the publications of the Eugenic Education Society, especially files of *The Eugenics Review*, London: 6 York Buildings, Adelphi.

53) Indiana has an admirable law on this subject, and New Jersey has just added the same to her statutes.

54) See *Statistics of Marriage and Divorce*, prepared by the Bureau

of the Census, beginning in 1906 and published in 1910.

55) *The Century of the Child,* New York: G P Putnam's Sons, 1907; *Love and Marriage,* G P Putnam's Sons, 1911; *Love and Ethics,* New York: B W Huebsch, 1911.

56) See *Woman and Economics* by Charlotte Perkins Gilman, Boston: Small, Maynard & Co, 1898; and the writings of H G Wells.

57) Arnold Lorand, *Old Age Deferred: The Cause of Old Age and its Postponement by Hygienic and Therapeutic Measures,* F A Davis Co, 1911.

58) See *Report of the Department of Superintendence of the National Education Association,* 1912.